A gift from Author Steve Windsor

I0417213

NDN BONUSES INCLUDE:

✓ Four Part Story Structure Scrivener Starter File
✓ Four Part Story Structure MS Word Starter File
✓ FREE and Bargain Book Marketing Submission Site List
✓ *Nine Day Novel: Self-Editing* Bonus Videos
✓ And much more!

Two ways to get instant access to the bonuses and more

ONE - Simply enter your email on any of our free product pages at https://authorbasics.com/shop/ and click the "Download Now" button.

TWO - Avoid entering your email for each freebie you want by becoming a FREE member of Author Basics, our author training community, at https://authorbasics.com/join/
THEN Login at https://authorbasics.com/my-account/
VISIT the bonus blog category or https://authorbasics.com/shop/
ENJOY the freebies!

NINE DAY NOVEL

AUTHOR

PHOBIA

STEVE WINDSOR

Published by

Vixen

vixenink.com

::Disclaimer

VIXEN ink

NINE DAY NOVEL: AUTHOR-PHOBIA

A VIXEN ink book/Published by arrangement with the author

(Printed Version)
ISBN-13: 978-1514140970
ISBN-10: 1514140977

Dedicated to my Fellow Sucking Authors

To us authors and our irrational fears. May we suck less today than we did yesterday.

THE SUCKING TABLE OF CONTENTS

NINE DAY NOVEL: AUTHOR-PHOBIA

THE SUCKING INTRODUCTION

QUOTATION BOOKS SUCK

"I hate quotations. Tell me what you know." —
Ralph Waldo Emerson

I despise pithy little quotation books that paraphrase long-dead authors as if their perspective on writing from 300 years ago has any bearing or relation to your current author struggle . . . in a modern-day capitalistic and overly technological culture. So . . . I decided to write one of my own.

Yep, that's how this book's gonna go. Hang on!

ARE YOU A SUCKING WRITER?

Have you ever. . .

- Heard that little voice inside your head, whispering to you that your writing sucked?
- Simply felt too terrified to start writing anything?
- Wanted to write a story but couldn't think of anything to write about?

- Had the wind knocked out of your sails—been critiqued by a seemingly well-meaning person and decided that they were right and gave up?

- Read and read and read motivational books on writing only to end up more fearful afterward?

- Compared yourself to "successful" writers and decided that you'll never measure up?

- Asked yourself, "Who would care about my stories, anyway?"

If so, congratulations! You're a writer!

The only trouble is—at this stage in the game, if you're not writing yet because you're afraid, chances are you think you'll suck at it. Well, I'll tell you what no other motivational mushery book about becoming an author will tell you—**in the beginning . . . you *do* suck at it. We all do.** Did.

And all those authors you want to be just like? They did too.

Calm down, calm down!

Trust me, **there isn't a successful author out there who didn't suck when they first started**. And that's the entire point of this book. Getting past your fear is easiest if you simply accept that at the beginning of learning any new skill, everyone and anyone must start out as a rookie.

The good news is, fear is fixable.

You don't know it yet, but **every one of those feelings above**, including the fear that you'll suck, **means that you're a writer**. It's that simple.

Non-writers, or people who don't care about writing, couldn't care less about any of those things. "Meh, so what?" they'd say. Just being able to identify those feelings in yourself, means that you give a damn about writing. And that's a powerful force you can harness.

> *"Admitting you're a writer is half the battle. The easy half or the hard half is up for debate."* — **Steve Windsor** (Tweet this!)

But, if realizing you're a writer is half the battle, why don't we all just pick up pens or flip open laptops as fast as we can and start writing? **What are we so afraid of, anyway?**

As it turns out . . . plenty.

YOUR FIRST NOVEL WILL SUCK

If you're like I was, upon feeling the first inkling that you might like to write, that was the voice you heard. A nagging voice that assured you that you wouldn't be any good at it.

The little critic in your head—every "sensible" person you'd ever known—extended its pinkie finger a little straighter, took another sip of that dry martini he was sipping (my critic's a "he"—kinda Thurston Howell III from Gilligan's Island). . .

Anyway, "Thurston" plucked that little plastic sword out of his glass. Then, bare-teethed, he bit down and slipped the salty, vodka-saturated olive off it. Then he ground it to a pulp in his mouth. After swallowing, he paused only briefly before he said, "Steve, you're not a writer. That's simply ridiculous!"

> *"If you hear a voice within you say 'you cannot paint,' then by all means paint, and that voice will be silenced."* — **Vincent Van Gogh**

If you remember nothing else from this book, remember that quote—it's the essence of how to overcome your fear of writing.

I wish I would've known that though, because instead I did what many of us do—most of us, in fact—I simply buried my desires to write . . . for almost 30 years.

I KNOW THAT SUCKING FEELING

That was when I was nineteen, and I made the mistake of showing a little story I had written to a girl I liked and she laughed at it. And that, as they say, was that.

Yeah. . . "No more writing," said Thurston. "Bad, bad idea." My testosterone-fueled, nineteen-year-old, "this is not gonna get a girl to like us" ego agreed—a scoffing chuckle was not the response we were looking for.

But I did write. If your soul wants something, your "brain" can't just tell it to shut up.

If you're a writer, your heart won't stop longing to write just because you're afraid. It'll chirp at you in the back of your mind, make you hang out in bookstores on Friday nights, cause you to read books on writing until you're blue in the face. The only thing it won't let you do— more accurately your fear won't let you do—is write.

The harder I tried to hold it in, the more the fire to write overflowed Thurston and my "brain's" ability to throw martinis and urgency on the flames to douse them.

I wrote poems, songs, love letters. Maybe those would work? And later in life as a technology professional, I wrote little stories, business ideas, slogans, titles, domain names. . . I wrote anything and everything.

Quarterly reports that read like *Game of Thrones* blood baths (because most of the startups I worked for were). And I wrote romantic poems that my inner embarrassed ego still wants to burn, but I can't bring myself to trash any of my many notepads full of hand-scrawled notes.

Yes, I still wrote, but from then on, only to myself.

Why?

FEAR OF SUCKING IS THE ENEMY

Why did I keep my writing to myself?

That one's easy—we all have it—the fear that I would suck.

Since the dawn of fire, man has understood, "Fire—hot. Don't touch." So, my psyche had a burned-in understanding that writing brought ridicule. Best to leave that lion caged up. And that I did . . . for far too long.

It was both an elation and a sad realization when I finally let that lion out of its cage. In the nick of time, most likely. I don't know how your writer voice can remain wild and beastly while locked up for so long, but now that the lion's out of the cage, it's roaring and it feels great! And that feeling is what I want to help you find.

Busting through your fear any way you have to—it's as easy and as monumentally difficult as deciding that's what it will take.

I wrote this book to help you plow through the fear that stops all of us from writing when the dream first occurs to us. And I wrote it so that the *process* of reading it actually makes you smile, and in some cases even laugh. Because **at the root of conquering any fear is the ability to find humor in that fear** . . . and then use that humor to overcome it.

Get ready to embrace the suck!

That's what it took for me, along with some seriously hard work. But the absolute elation at doing something I loved for a change helped too. So . . . what's it gonna take for you?

For me, it took a lot. **Fear is arguably the most powerful human emotion to overcome**. After years and years of letting my will to write bubble and boil below the surface, I finally decided that enough was enough.

That's a little white lie, though.

In reality, what had to happen was that I had to come so close to being burned. . . So near the flames of total failure, that I figured writing couldn't suck any worse than what I was already going through. It took me getting as low as I was willing to go, to finally turn and face the fear. You probably don't want to hear that story—too ugly.

What? You still wanna know? Train wrecks—we all want to watch them.

Hmmm. . . Let's just say that after a company I started with family members failed—yeah, who knew that was a bad idea, right?—my wife and I moved back to the Bay Area in California. Then I spent a year interviewing for jobs at companies like Google and other Silicon Valley powerhouses. Management positions that just three years before, I would've landed easily. . . As an aging technology director in Silicon Valley, if you haven't become a VP by 45. . .

So, a year of that and the "writing" was on the wall—there would be no six-figure salary to help pay California's exorbitant rents and real estate prices.

Luckily, my wife landed a job before things got ugly. But per diem ICU nursing was far from stable and so neither of us thought it was a good idea to leave our "temporary" housing—living with our two daughters in extra rooms at her parents' house until we both got jobs. Oh . . . I didn't tell you about that?

I looked in the mirror and realized I sucked.

If you've never tasted that kind of failure—witnessed that kind of self-induced self-criticism in a mirror each morning, trying to gather the energy to lift your toothbrush, let alone shave—then you've never before gone from upper middle class to unemployed, unemployable, un-empowered and any other "un" you can think of. "Thurston" was quick to point out that we had indeed . . . failed . . . miserably.

I could see Hell from my window.

A year of sarcastically calling myself the "manny" for our two lovely daughters, plunging into an unhealthy, unhappy and unkempt lethargy of lunacy and lackadaisical lament. . . Not to mention the ever-present cocktail-party question du jour, "What do you do [for a living]?" . . . "Oh, I sponge off of my wife's hard work, drive kids to and from whatever, over-consume coffee, cook and sometimes clean, but not as much as my wife would like, and, in general . . . I suck."

At that point, whoever was doing the obligatory courtesy of chit-chatting me would roll their eyes into the back of their head and they'd try one more time: "Ahhh, I . . . I see," they'd say. "Well"—the pause was so they could contemplate running—"well, where do you live?"

It was a question that I'm sure they figured would be safe and maybe hurry their obviously pointless social-networking efforts to a more productive pasture. But when someone deadpans an answer back like, "With my mother-in-law," I mean, seriously, where do you go from there?

Quickly, they'd introduce me to the gardeners working in the back yard, probably in hopes that I would have more economically and socially in common with them and be able to provide better party banter. Secretly we both knew —that kind of suck? You don't want to get any of *that* "on" you—if you know what I mean.

THE BEGINNING . . . SUCKS

You can use failure to propel you forward.

Another six months or so of that—the shock therapy has since helped remove much of those years from my memory, but you can only take so much voltage—and I was just about done with. . .

Yeah, I hate it when I lie, too.

So, my wife was tired of me staying up until 3 a.m. to re-watch HBO's *The Wire*, failing to shower (I really didn't see the point), and my generally surly attitude. . . I guess she figured if I was going to act like a grizzled old author recluse, I might as well get paid for it.

Ever the optimist, my wife finally said, "You keep saying you want to write a novel." She has a nasty habit of walking right to the center of a self-pitying mud hole that I want to wallow in and paving over any excuse I might offer up. "Why don't you just do it? You've got the time."

Was that a jab at us being unemployed? Thurston asked inside my head. *Did she just say we suck? The absolute nerve of it!*

Of course it was a jab. We don't have time to. . . There's the laundry to do—

Okay, I already said I wasn't doing any laundry, but the dishes. . . Okay, I wasn't doing dishes either. Or the—

"Tomorrow morning," my wife interrupted my thoughts, "I'm giving you all day to go to Peets [coffeehouse] and write. You don't have to do anything else."

She's an absolute lunatic! Thurston said. *We'll not be told what to do!*

I agreed with Thurston—too much going on.

> *"My wife gave me a year to start making money*

out of writing, and after six months, I'd made not a bean. Suddenly, the books took off, and the beans started coming in!" — **Jonathan Stroud**

The reality—my wife knew it too—was an irrational but debilitating fear of sucking, plain and simple. If I went to write in the morning, there would be no going back—no more excuses. No more wondering if I had missed the boat of my life and no more ability to say that I "couldn't" before I'd even tried.

Thurston made me give false apathy one last try anyway. "But I could care less about—"

"But nothing," my wife said. "Go down there and just do it. You're good at that—**any time you give a crap about something, you're good at it**. That's who you are. So go down and do it."

Goddammit, said Thurston, *she's using logic! Stop her!*

> *"Sometimes the knowledge that someone else believes in us is more important than believing in ourselves."* — **Steve Windsor** (Tweet This!)

Whoa! Way too early in this book for a philosophical quote. Let's move on.

WHAT THE SUCK AM I DOING?

Still, where do you start? I was no author, and worse, I was sure I would suck.

> *"You can fix anything but a blank page."* — **Nora Roberts**

But the next morning, I paid for my mocha, sat down at a corner table inside my favorite coffeehouse, and pulled out my laptop. I stared at a blank Word document. (This was before I discovered the beauty of Scrivener.) "This is going to suck" was the only thought in my head. I had no idea what to write. . .

> *"In a very real sense, the writer writes in order to teach himself, to understand himself."* — **Alfred Kazin**

But if I had no idea what I was doing, then what *should* I do? A thought struck me, but I hesitated. For a brief moment, my fear took all the give-a-crap that I'd mustered right out of me. But a few sips of coffee later, and I was ready to figure things out. And my idea came back: *I'll write to myself.*

> *"Better to write for yourself and have no public, than to write for the public and have no self."* — **Cyril Connolly**

Hmmm. . . I would find out later that this old dude's wisdom was not the conventional commercial view on marketing your writing.

Yet, the thought persisted. What would it be like, instead of sucking, to be the best version of myself I could be? What would I tell myself? If I came back from the future, what would I tell my "suck-self" about what it would take to win at this? Because I was sick of sucking.

Then another thought hit me. . .

> *"Ideas are like rabbits. You get a couple and learn how to handle them, and pretty soon you have a dozen."* — **John Steinbeck**

I remembered a book I'd read a few years earlier called *Conversations With God*. Yes, I realize—yet another in a long list of irreconcilable ironies that plague me. Honestly, considering my thoughts on religion, I certainly write about it often enough.

Regardless, in that book, Neale Donald Walsch, the reforming downtrodden alcoholic author looking for answers, asked God questions about his own life and life in general, and then, ostensibly, "God" . . . answered him back.

Now, since they didn't spike that author to a cross for

purporting to be the next coming of Jesus Christ or Moses, I can hardly attest to the truth or validity of the contents of his book, but that concept was there and it had popped into my head for a reason.

Ask yourself a question, get an answer, an honest one. So that's exactly what I did.

My first question was, "What am I doing?" Because I was clueless.

Three days and 40,000 words later, and my "suck"-self and my "super"-self had enjoyed one of the longest conversations I could remember having with anyone.

Forget that any normal person would've been checked into a mental institution had the written words been spoken aloud instead, but I had physically typed 40,000 words . . . in three days! And better still, somewhere along the way I'd forgotten to worry about those words sucking.

The voices in your head are real.

During the entire process, there were two distinct voices in my head as I typed—one that whined and made excuses, and one that told that whiner to grab his package, get real and get going.

I found later that therein lies the core of all writing and fiction storytelling in particular: You have to harness every "version" of yourself in order to write.

Don't take my word for it.

> *"Whether we are describing a king, an assassin, a thief, an honest man, a prostitute, a nun, a young girl, or a stallholder in a market, it is always ourselves that we are describing."* — **Guy De Maupassant**

Back to my 40,000 words of suck.

Those 40,000 words are very personal, very honest and so brutally private that they'll never see the self-published light of day. So why do it at all? Why type 40,000 words for nothing?

> *"Word count matters. Whether you throw it away or not."* —**Steve Windsor** (Tweet This!)

Forget that I didn't realize when you find a subject that your fingers can't type fast enough to follow your own thoughts, you've struck writer's block-busting gold, but **not all writing should be published or read**. That's like making a bodybuilding competition judge witness every one of Arnold Schwarzenegger's workouts.

Some writing is simply meant to grow the muscle for the real show.

Write . . . to learn.

> *"First, I do not sit down at my desk to put into verse something that is already clear in my mind. If it were clear in my mind, I should have no incentive or need to write about it. We do not write in order to be understood; we write in order to understand."* — **Cecil Day-Lewis**

One of the best pieces of advice I read after my decision to become a writer, was to **write about something that you desperately want to learn**. In doing that, the theory goes, you'll inevitably do the research and the hard work necessary to become enough of an "expert" on the subject that your legitimacy is assured. In Latin it's called ipso facto—by the fact itself.

Whatever you do . . . you are.

It gives you the end result. Research and writing produces confidence and understanding of the subject matter. And it was at that point that a little voice in my head . . . started to believe.

Now, of course, Thurston threw a martini in that little voice's eye, told it that he sucked, and sent him away crying. That feeling of belief turned back to doubt and self-criticism rather quickly.

But one thing that I had learned in twenty years of reading three-inch-thick books to understand technology, was that momentum and doing have infinite power. It takes a lot of energy to get a locomotive moving, but once you do it's almost impossible to stop.

Let's hammer this point home with a little Latin, shall we?

> Vires acquirit eundo — *"It gains strength by going."*
> — **Virgil**

Anyway, there I was—40,000 words of Steve said-the "other" Steve said, back-and-forth dialogue blather. In hindsight, punctuated piss-poorly, in my now-author opin-ion. So, what to do next?

As I read the words—because you know you have to read the blather that your super-self told your suck-self—I realized that suck-self . . . sucked at punctuating dialogue. So guess what? I had to go research how dialogue was punctuated. And I did.

And a funny thing happened on the way to the persona store to buy myself a non-sucking author avatar. . .

Now, keep in mind that a few days prior, I had no clue

what to do next in my life, no direction or give-a-shit to find one, and no idea that writing would have anything to do with the solution once I gave a crap about figuring it out. But I was unwittingly doing one of the most essential parts of becoming an author—**I put on the blinders, stopped worrying about the entire process** and instead **dealt with what was in front of my face** . . . at that moment.

> *"Your job as an author is to write the next word. No more. No less."* — **Steve Windsor** (Tweet This!)

And *at* that moment, all I knew—all I was focused on—was that my dialogue and its punctuation needed to be fixed.

So research I did—momentum I'd started. (Was that Yoda?)

MY WRITER VOICE . . . SUCKS

That last statement is as good a time as any to introduce you to my "writer voice."

In *Nine Day Novel: Outlining*, *NDN: Writing* and *NDN: Self-Editing*, I talk about some hardcore, probably uncomfortable "methods" that I use to pump words onto the page. After getting countless emails from budding authors who were obviously struggling to simply get past that fear-laden "I'll suck" phase, I decided that a little tongue-in-cheek suck-bashing would do all of us some good.

I'm guessing that this book is one of many you've bought to help you figure out how to become an author. **But what a lot of books skip over, in my opinion, is the lunacy of our fears when we first start out.**

There are tons of writing books being published every day. We could use a little bit more of the reality behind our own fears and how to overcome them. I find that poking fun at and being irreverent toward irrational fears helps people understand their own struggles better. It's kind of a "laugh out loud in a dark graveyard at night" strategy.

If you're like me, you finally broke through your fear and started your author journey—ahem—*later* in life than you should have. And I've said in my other books that because of that, I don't have extra time to play nice-nice and fool around pontificating my motivation. I feel like I have to catch up.

I got a little extra time on my hands.

That being said, young Jedi, as it turns out, recently, I found a little "extra" time I forgot about, buried beneath the junk in my garage, so I thought it might be fun to play nice-nice and fool around pontificating our motivation for a little while.

So, ready or not, my "Darth Vader"-style kick in the butt will now turn its lightsaber on the funny bone. And if you're struggling with finding the "force" to write—waking up your inner-Princess Leia or Luke Skywalker Jedi author—you've come to the right place.

However, **forgive me if I offend your delicate sensibilities, but my "voice" isn't for everyone**. For some people, dare I say, my voice sucks. But I'm sensing you're the kind of author who "gets" me, so if that's the case, I'm the kind of coach who'll "challenge" you to overcome your inner suck.

And I mean this with all sincerity when I say, may this farce of a book be with you. ;-)

SUCK BUSTER:

If you're not careful, this book's gonna grind on your nerves. But that's exactly what I want it to do. Because I like the anger—a dash of "pissed-off," if you will. A lot of times that's just what the doctor prescribed to blast past your fear.

Here's an example:

It's actually kinda fitting that I have an Emilio Estevez quote in this book, because the parable I'll relate is from one of his movies.

The Mighty Ducks was a movie about a haphazard group of hockey kids who ended up being taught to win by an even worse-off formerly-hopeful hockey player, turned reluctant coach—Emilio Estevez. (Wait, that . . . that seems a familiar tale. . .)

In that movie, the goalie, Goldberg, was afraid of getting hit by the puck. So Emilio tied him to the goal and had the team shoot pucks at him until he realized that they didn't hurt. That *and* the realization that he'd lost his fear of being hit.

That's exactly what I'm going to do with you and your fear of the word "suck." Now, since I can't tie you to a goal, I'll just tell you that you do *not* want me to use my voodoo doll if you put this book down. You'll see what I mean later.

SUCKING THE "TO" OUT OF HOW-TO

To those of you who've read my other books, you know I like to get down and dirty pretty fast—get to the "how" in how-to. With this book, I vowed to get to that "how" as fast as I could, and then let you enjoy the "mushery" after-wards if you so desired.

So, if I had to boil down every motivational and instructional book on becoming an author that I've ever read, especially the ones about becoming a *self-published* author. . . and if I had to summarize my experience on that journey, this is what I'd write:

- We're all afraid when we first start out.

- You *think* that the primary fear you have, is that you'll suck.

- That fear is actually the fear that others will tell you that your *writing* is terrible.

To overcome that fear:

- Figure out why you want to write. Write it down. Remember it, because every time you want to quit you have to go back and look at it.

- Realize that no matter what anyone tells you or how you try to hide it, a part of that reason is that you want to write for a living and that translates to making money. And there's *nothing* wrong with that.

- Declare yourself a writer, because if you write, you are. You don't need permission to do that. If you do, you officially have my permission. Write that down too—**"Steve gave me permission."**

Who am I to give you advice?

I'm nobody, but so was every other author . . . at one time or another. So I gave myself permission to share what I've learned with you during my own struggles. Yep, it's that simple. Is someone going to call me out on that? Most assuredly. Do I have some fear over it? Less and less every day.

Success starts . . . with suck.

- There's no way to say, "success" unless you start with "suck." The first syllable in "success" is "suck."

- Unfortunately, what most authors do at the first sign of trouble is quit. In short, they succumb. A very different word and outcome that starts with "suck."

- Many would-be writer-authors have bought into courses, advice, and information that gives them the false belief that succeeding at writing is "easy" or "quick." That they don't have to start at the suck. Those poor souls are called, you guessed it, "suckers."

This is the reality:

- In the beginning, you'll suck.

- Your job as an author . . . is to suck less.

- With each book you write, you will suck less.

- If you keep comparing your writing to other authors, *A-achoo—Stephen King*, you'll always suck.

- Compare your writing to what you wrote yesterday.

- "Suck" is a relative and subjective term.

- I'm here to help you get over the word "suck." Because what it really means is someone who's new at something. Like when cops call a new police officer a "rookie."

- What they really mean, trust me on this one, is that rookie sucks, because until he or she's done the job for a while, they do suck. That doesn't mean they're bad at it, that just means they're inexperienced.

- Since "inexperienced" is such a long word to type on an incident report, the police have all agreed to use the word "suck."

Some more sucking blasphemy.

- The first sentence Stephen King ever wrote . . . "sucked."

- All first drafts . . . suck.

- When you were first born into the world, all you did . . . was suck.

- Think about it—any new job you ever started, your first day . . . sucked.

- "Suck" doesn't necessarily mean bad.

"Courage is not the absence of fear, but—how did a pithy quote get in here?" — **Steve Windsor** (Tweet This!)

- Realize that everyone was afraid of rejection when they started, even the almighty Stephen King.

- Write down what you think makes you a unique snowflake of fear. There are a hundred people with that exact same fear.

- Action trumps fear—writing is the only thing that will get rid of the fear of criticism once you declare yourself an author. So take action and write.

- Find a community of other writers to share with. They're on Facebook, Twitter, Google Plus, websites and in virtually every major city.

- Build an author platform. No one really knows or defines what that is.

- An author platform is any service, system, website or strategy that funnels fans onto your email list so you can convey information and sell to them directly. Or I could be wrong. . .

- Learn the tools of the trade—software, systems, applications. Whether you use Word, Google Docs, Scrivener, or any other program, pick one . . . and get writing. (Yep, I'm biased, too.)

- Write with the purpose of creating valuable information for, or assisting or entertaining someone. Give away the best of that information, assistance or entertainment.

- Use that free stuff to build an email list of ferocious fans.

- Write *for* those fans to *get* more fans.

- Writing for a living is a marathon game and the quick successes you're seeing online took months and years despite what the "brochures" say.

- Writing is hard work just like any other job.

- Carve out time to write every day if you can, every week if you can't, or take thirty straight days and write dawn to dusk. The point?

- Figure out how to wrap your lifestyle and life around writing. There are many ways to do that. Your way will be different from the "only" way they say it can be done.

- That "only" way "they" say it can be done is to write 500-1000 words per day every day. Good advice for some, total shit for others.

"Your writing voice is the deepest possible reflection of who you are. The job of your voice is not to seduce or flatter or make well-shaped sentences. In your voice, your readers should be able to hear the contents of your mind, your heart, your soul." — **Meg Rosoff**

- Rip off your filter, don't censor yourself. Write raw, authentic and real. Use your own writing voice—it's the only one that matters.

- Realize that the first draft of anything you write will suck. Write it anyway, then read it out loud and rewrite it.

- Hire a professional editor. Self-edit your work before and after it goes to the editor.

- Get professional book covers made.

- Learn how to self-publish. Skip "publishing" because you're wasting your time. Later, once you've built your platform—fans and following and books—a publisher will be more receptive to your inquiries. By then, you won't need them.

- Don't wait—self-publish quickly, before the fear can stop you.

- Once you click "publish," stop incessantly watching your sales statistics.

- Reality? You're going to incessantly watch your sales statistics.

"Self-publishing is like throwing blood in the ocean. Not long before a critic shows up." — **Steve Windsor** (Tweet this!)

- Understand that critics will find you.

- No matter what anyone says, criticism sucks. Write anyway.

- Most criticism is about the critic, not you.

- That won't make you feel any better about it.

"It troubles me that people speak about writing for money as ugly and distasteful." — **Joyce Maynard**

- Don't kid yourself—you wanna make some money.

- Writing is a business and you have to build a brand around yourself. Write insanely useful information or entertainment to build that brand.

- Learn about the business of writing and self-publishing by reading books and taking on-line courses and connecting with other authors any way you can.

- Persevere in the face of a short-term lack of results. Write more.

- Enjoy every success no matter how small. Realize that success is the result of hard work. Do the hard work . . . or don't.

- Your definition of "success" is just over the horizon—your next book. Write that next book.

- Rinse . . . Repeat.

Well, now that that's over with, I guess you *can* put this book down. Unless of course, you want to have a little fun.

THE SUCKING BONUSES

NINE DAY NOVEL SUCKING BONUSES

I wanted to make the *Nine Day Novel* series bonuses as valuable, if not more valuable, than the books themselves. I've packed in things like a Four Part Story Structure Scrivener starter file, self-editing tutorial videos, outlining Scrivener starter files and more.

SUCK BUSTER:

Take a minute to get instant access to all of the bonus materials for the *Nine Day Novel* series.

If you skipped the bonus offer page at the start of this book, here's how you access the bonuses.

Step 1 - become a FREE member of Author Basics at https://authorbasics.com/join

Step 2 - Go to the "Bonuses" blog category section at https://authorbasics.com/bonus-content/ or go to the product page of any one of our free products at https://authorbasics.com/shop/ and immediately "suck" . . . less!

IDENTIFYING THE SUCKING ENE-MY

ENOUGH SUCKING AROUND

Vitanda est improba siren desidia — **Horace**
"One must avoid that wicked temptress, Laziness."

Careful, or this could happen. . .

*"Where is this wicked temptress 'Laziness'? She
sounds divine—I must stop writing and meet her."*
Steve Windsor — (Tweet this!)

I've been called a lot of things in my life. "Lazy" isn't one
of them. If I could tell you to cultivate one strength in your
character that will serve you as a successful author, it
would be to exercise and viciously grow your will to
work . . . hard. This and this alone may be all you'll need
to defeat the suck.

Fun finishes fear!

Summing up this book could be as simple as telling you
that becoming an author—getting over your fear of writing
—is hard work. Yet, I've found the best way to help people

understand something—overcome their fears of it—is to wrap the entire big ball of black fear . . . inside some fun.

YOU'VE LOST THAT SUCKING FEELING

Top Gun. Love that song!

Back to my suck.

I scoured Google, I bought ebooks, I researched and read everything I could about fiction dialogue and its punctuation. And then you know what I did . . . with that 40,000 words I knew I wasn't ever going to publish? I started self-editing it.

Word by word, line by line and page by sucking page, I fixed mistakes. I put commas where they were supposed to be, I closed open-ended quotations and I separated my two characters' dialogue into correct paragraphs. I even slipped in some action beats and exposition once I learned what those were.

When I got stuck, I researched more and learned more and then I got back at it and did more. And I drank coffee and I forgot to eat, and got a sore ass from sitting in a coffeehouse chair.

But along the way, a beautiful thing was happening—**I was falling in love with the mechanics of writing and I**

was completely forgetting to worry about whether or not I sucked. It was clear I did and there was only one way to fix that problem. . .

The bits and pieces of writing were something I could grab onto—familiar trail markers that the writing "gods" had left behind as breadcrumbs for us sucky authors to find. Clues to use, so we might actually string words together and write with the intention of telling stories that didn't suck. It was marvelous!

Writing had some rules, tools and old fools I could follow! Holy sucking Hallelujah!

RULES? YOU'RE SUCKING KIDDING ME?

Now, those of you who've read any of my books know that if I say the "R" word (rules) without pausing to spit on the sidewalk first, something's amiss. But here's what a few old dead authors have to say about them:

> *"Rules are a point to build a story around. They are a plain, solid, square foundation. If you stick to that foundation, you get a solid, plain, square building. Nothing wrong with it, but nothing notable either. To make an interesting building, you've got to go beyond that foundation, ignoring it as much as you can without having the building fall apart. The bending of the rules until the story is*

ready to crumble is what makes a good story— interesting, intriguing, and plausible, but almost ready to burst." — **David Morrow**

Okay, there are rules and by learning those rules, you'll have the power to understand how to break them. Thus ensuring that your writing will begin to suck less. I was loving learning the facts about writing.

"Look behind the curtain of any magic show and what you'll find is hours and hours of practicing the mechanics of misdirection and slight-of-hand. Seeming "tricks"—actions—performed so infinitely and then so eloquently as to make them seem like mystical sorcery, unrepeatable by anyone but a true master magician." — **Steve Windsor**

Or, if you don't like the way I say it. . .

"There's no 'magic secret'; writing is like every-thing else; ten percent inspiration or talent, and ninety percent hard work. Persistence; keeping at it till you get there." — **Marion Zimmer Bradley**

Practice and you'll suck less. Got it.

"Writing has laws of perspective, of light and shade, just as painting does, or music. If you are born knowing them, fine. If not, learn them. Then

rearrange the rules to suit yourself." — **Truman Capote**

More practice. Ditto. . .

You want to know how to win a game? Start out by learning all there is to know about the rules. Then, once you've mastered that, prepare to expand the boundaries and win by bending the rules where they need to be, breaking them when you can get away with it.

You don't have to be immortal to do that.

SKIPPING THE SUCK

But what about my fear? You're skipping right past it.

Ah yes, that nagging fear.

It's my guess that you'll be like I was and if you can simply get started. . .

During the entire time that I immersed myself in the act of typing physical words onto a virtual page on my computer, my mind was too busy making my fingers move, and during my research my brain was too busy solving my dialogue problems, that **my fear didn't have the space to make itself heard**.

Crowding out fear

I said it before, my fear of sucking simply got crowded out by work that had to be done.

Fingers had to move, questions had to be answered and rules had to be learned so they could be broken. That left no place to wonder what would come of it all. My mind simply embraced the idea that what mattered was the learning. Not the not-sucking, but the succeeding.

Therapy is expensive. Writing is cheap.

There's a side benefit to all this. Writing, as it turns out, is great therapy.

> *"Writing is a form of therapy; sometimes I wonder how all those who do not write, compose or paint can manage to escape the madness, melancholia, the panic fear which is inherent in a human situation."* — **Graham Greene**

Um, don't ask me how I know this, but therapy is some expensive . . . well, therapy. Wait, I can explain. It wasn't *that* kind of therapy. Oh, dammit—I suck.

> *"Every secret of a writer's soul, every experience of his life, every quality of his mind is written large in his works."* — **Virginia Woolf**

Translation? You can talk to a professional about your irrational fear of writing for around $125 an hour, or you can write about it and turn it into awesome books that one day may make you rich and famous. The goal either way will be the same—exercising demons.

Fear is the biggest demon of them all. But fear can be conquered by facing it head-on. Here's what one of my favorite inspirational authors has to say about it:

> *"Write what disturbs you, what you fear, what you have not been willing to speak about. Be willing to be split open."* — **Natalie Goldberg**

I'm not sure about that "splitting open" part, but the rest. . . At 47, I had amassed a considerable amount to "speak" about.

If you want to write a novel, and even if you just think you want to write one, skip the fear that you'll suck part.

I'm not trivializing it. Here's how you're going to do it.

SUCK BUSTER:

Don't plan on showing your first novel to anyone.

What? That's right.

We're going to skip the fear part by negating what's really causing it—the fear of rejection. So your very first effort—I give you permission—you're not going to show the results to anyone. That's right, this one's gonna be for practice, so there's absolutely no risk of someone saying it sucks.

"Geez, Steve, writing an entire novel that no one's going to read? That sounds like a whole lot of hard work for nothing. I mean, I don't have the time for—"

Oh, Darth-dammit! The voice trails off in my head and I slowly slip my lightsaber from my belt. Vmmmmmm. . . The shaft lights up to a red-hot electric glow and the voice stops. The saber always gets their attention. If it doesn't. . . Well, there was little hope in the first place.

When learning a new skill, hard work is the only path.

> *"Any man who keeps working is not a failure. He may not be a great writer, but if he applies the old-fashioned virtues of hard, constant labor, he'll eventually make some kind of career for himself as writer."* – **Ray Bradbury**

And the best way to start is to start learning.

Do the research and the hard work. Learn like you were

starting a new career or a new job, or reading the manual for a new car you just bought. You do that, right?

Okay, maybe I'm the only one who reads car manuals, but that's one of the reasons I can drive better than any other motorist on the road. Yes, except you, of course.

Every discipline, be it gardening or galaxy gazing, has instructions you can follow. Writing has rules just like a game of soccer does. Structures and forms and compositions that you can learn, and the best part—all that stuff is written down in books that you can buy for ridiculously low prices. You don't have to go to a university to become a writer. Some of the best writers in history never did.

As an author, all promotion is self-promotion.

You want to learn about how to write a novel? I've written several books about the very basic mechanics of fiction storytelling to help you do just that.

Are they the best books out there? Are anyone's? I'll tell you what they are—damned simple to understand, follow and learn from. And in the beginning, style and muse and character arcs and inner journeys and feelings and mushery don't put words on the paper that you can practice with and improve. They'll just confuse you. So, here's my suggestion:

SELF-SERVING SUCK BUSTER:

The basics of fiction writing:

Step 1 - Read *Nine Day Novel: Self-Editing*—the second half of the book. It's **packed full of basic fiction dialogue, exposition and action beat structures** to help you understand how fiction sentences are constructed and punctuated.

Step 2 - Read *Nine Day Novel: Outlining*. It will walk you through the process I use to **go from no idea at all to outlining and filling in the action beats for an entire fiction novel**. It's full of examples and different ways to explain the standard Four Part Story Structure.

Step 3 - Read *Nine Day Novel: Writing Fiction*. It's my take on **carving out time to hammer words onto the page** as fast as I can to produce an editable draft. It also details and gives examples of the **Four Part Story Structure to help you create a hero's journey** that's interesting to readers.

Don't worry, if that's too much to tackle right now, we're still going to explore those fears and bust through some of the suck about becoming an author in the next chapter.

THIS LIST OF FEARS SUCKS

Fear is a useful tool.

Let's say you want to have a child, keep them safe for the eighteen years it'll take to get them ready to face the world and fend for themselves, and you want to get them there with a modest belief that they'll be able to handle things on their own. Well, as it turns out, one of the tools in your arsenal as a parent . . . will be fear.

The double-edged sword of fear

Fear is useful and immediate when, say, you don't want your child to get run over by a bus. So you prevent him or her from crossing the street without looking. And the immediate results, by instilling a healthy amount of fear of a busy intersection to achieve that, are undeniable.

However, as a society, we've gone a little bit overboard in applying fear to nearly every situation and sin we can think of.

> *"If you have an important point to make, don't try to be subtle or clever. Use a pile driver. Hit the point once. Then come back and hit it again. Then hit it a third time—a tremendous whack!"* — **Winston Churchill**

One person's fear is another's funfest.

"It's never appropriate to make fun of people's fears. . . So, when you find you have no choice, it's best to use a fictitious character to do that dirty work for you." — **Steve Windsor**

Cut to Darth—

By the time we're out of high school, we've been exposed to so many fears that it's remarkable we aren't all carted off to campuses with security blankets and pacifiers still swinging on ribbons from little chip-clips attached to our bibs. (If you're a parent, you know exactly what the "chip-clip" thing is. If not . . . if you become a parent, you will.)

Let's laundry-list all these fears. Take a deep breath. . .

Top 100 fears in order of prevalence in modern society:

1. **Arachnophobia** – The fear of spiders. Seriously, Peter Parker is not that scary.

2. **Ophidiophobia** – The fear of snakes. Harrison Ford ripoff alert: Snakes. . . Why does it always have to be snakes?

3. **Acrophobia** – The fear of heights. Eiffel Tower—off the bucket list.

4. **Agoraphobia** – The fear of open or crowded spaces. If you've got it bad, you won't leave

home. Pizza delivery for dinner again.

5. **Cynophobia** – The fear of dogs. In my defense, I was bitten as a kid, so . . . death to dogs! Not the cute cuddly puppy ones, of course.

6. **Astraphobia** – The fear of thunder and lightning. This one's loud and clear.

7. **Claustrophobia** – The fear of small spaces. Does this page feel small to you?

8. **Mysophobia** – The fear of germs. I leave this one to my wife—ICU nurse.

9. **Aerophobia** – The fear of flying on airplanes. How many airplane movies does it take for this one to crash and burn into your long-term memory?

10. **Trypophobia** – The fear of holes. Not touching this one.

11. **Carcinophobia** – The fear of cancer. The marketing campaign for this one warrants it being higher on the list.

12. **Thanatophobia** – The fear of death. Um, these are getting a bit obvious.

13. **Glossophobia** – The fear of public speaking. This is the "steak and potatoes" of fears.

14. **Monophobia** – The fear of being alone. They had me at "mono." I got this cold, lonely

feeling.

15. **Atychiphobia** – The fear of failure. Highlight this one.

16. **Ornithophobia** – The fear of birds. Damn you, Alfred Hitchcock!

17. **Alektorophobia** – The fear of chickens. This is a fear? What the cluck?

18. **Enochlophobia** – The fear of crowds. As we approach ten billion people on the planet, I expect this one to get worse.

19. **Aphenphosmphobia** – The fear of intimacy. It's not so much the intimacy as the byproduct that scares me.

20. **Trypanophobia** – The fear of needles. If you go in the Army, you'll get over this one fast—I've never been stuck so many times.

21. **Anthropophobia** – The fear of people. I'd say "certain" people.

22. **Aquaphobia** – The fear of water. Witches have this one bad.

23. **Autophobia** – The fear of abandonment. Not even remotely. I need a Tom Hanks *Cast Away* island to write from.

24. **Hemophobia** – The fear of blood. Only my own . . . leaving my body.

25. **Gamophobia** – The fear of commitment. It's

the "for life" part that's . . . troubling.

26. **Hippopotomonstrosesquippedaliophobia**
– The fear of long words. Just the size of that
word gave me feelings of . . . inadequacy.

27. **Xenophobia** – The fear of the unknown. It
scares me that I didn't know this one.

28. **Vehophobia** – The fear of driving. Have you
seen the traffic out there?

29. **Basiphobia** – The fear of falling. Once
again, some pretty instinctual stuff.

30. **Achievemephobia** – The fear of success.
Yeah, when I get there, I'll hire a therapist to
get me over this one.

31. **Theophobia** – The fear of God. I think religion's delivering this message loud and
clear.

32. **Ailurophobia** – The fear of cats. Only the
ones that aren't smashed on the freeway.
Okay, okay—I'm trying to lie, but it's just not
working.

33. **Metathesiophobia** – The fear of change. I
could use more change, actually.

34. **Globophobia** – The fear of balloons. Only
the scary clowns holding them.

35. **Nyctophobia** – The fear of darkness. One
word—nightlight.

36. **Androphobia** – The fear of men. I'm teaching this one to my daughters.

37. **Phobophobia** – The fear of fear. This one just scares the fear right out of me.

38. **Philophobia** – The fear of love. Do I have this one? Can't say I do. (That's a . . . a marriage pun.)

39. **Triskaidekaphobia** – The fear of the number 13. Elevators don't have it.

40. **Emetophobia** – The fear of vomiting. Actually, after a bad Cinco de Mayo tequila binge . . . I welcome it.

41. **Gephyrophobia** – The fear of bridges. Only the ones that collapse.

42. **Entomophobia** – The fear of bugs and insects. I thought we covered this with Peter Parker?

43. **Lepidopterophobia** – The fear of butterflies. One Monarch of a fear, right there.

44. **Panophobia** – The fear of everything. True story: I was once having a conversation with my brother's wife and she said, "There are only two things that I'm really afraid of—" I had to interrupt her. I smiled and said, "Yeah, everything . . . and everything else." Some jokes are just . . . misunderstood.

45. **Podophobia** – The fear of feet. Two words—

foot rub.

46. **Paraskevidekatriaphobia** – The fear of Friday the 13th. My friend Jason in Texas doesn't have this.

47. **Somniphobia** – The fear of sleep. Only when it cuts into my writing time.

48. **Gynophobia** – The fear of women. I never caught this one.

49. **Apiphobia** – The fear of bees. Bee stings hurt. Enough said.

50. **Koumpounophobia** – The fear of buttons. I could say something here, but I'm swearing off of sexual in-your-endos for the year.

51. **Anatidaephobia** – The fear that somewhere in the world, a duck is watching you. What . . . the duck?

52. **Pyrophobia** – The fear of fire. Thank God for cavemen.

53. **Ranidaphobia** – The fear of frogs. This one makes me wanna croak. (See . . . that's a double entendre—never mind.)

54. **Galeophobia** – The fear of sharks. Once again, stating the obvious?

55. **Athazagoraphobia** – The fear of forgetting. How would you remember if you had this?

56. **Katsaridaphobia** – The fear of cockroaches.

Only those New York ones.

57. **Iatrophobia** – The fear of doctors. They make you sick, ya know.

58. **Pediophobia** – The fear of dolls. One movie character—Chucky from the *Child's Play* series.

59. **Ichthyophobia** – The fear of fish. Jesus had a tough time with this one.

60. **Achondroplasiaphobia** – The fear of midgets. After *Game of Thrones*, I kinda like them now.

61. **Mottephobia** – The fear of moths. They keep eating my sweaters.

62. **Zoophobia** – The fear of animals. San Diego Zoo, anyone?

63. **Bananaphobia** – The fear of bananas. One long fear that I'm not touching.

64. **Sidonglobophobia** – The fear of cotton balls. Ditto—not touching them.

65. **Scelerophobia** – The fear of crime. This one's just a ripoff.

66. **Cibophobia** – The fear of food. I wish.

67. **Phasmophobia** – The fear of ghosts. Yeah, because they're spooky. Duh!

68. **Equinophobia** – The fear of horses. Only that really old talking Mr. Ed one.

69. **Musophobia** – The fear of mice. Cinderella got over hers.

70. **Catoptrophobia** – The fear of mirrors. I guess if you're not the fairest, then this one's inevitable.

71. **Agliophobia** – The fear of pain. This one really hurts.

72. **Tokophobia** – The fear of pregnancy. This . . . is possibly my worst fear. Every time I go in a hot tub I'm like, "Careful. . . Careful. . ."

73. **Telephonophobia** – The fear of talking on the phone. My wife does not have this one . . . at all.

74. **Pogonophobia** – The fear of beards. Aw, poor Hagrid.

75. **Omphalophobia** – The fear of belly buttons. Honestly, when people tell me they have this one, I just wanna tell them to go contemplate their navel. (Okay, that one was lame.)

76. **Pseudodysphagia** – The fear of choking. Kwai Chang Caine doesn't have this. (This one gets obscurity bonus points. If you figure it out, email me, because your mind's twisted enough to read my novels.)

77. **Bathophobia** – The fear of depths. Every time I take BART under the San Francisco

Bay. Oooh . . . that gives me an idea for a novel!

78. **Cacomorphobia** – The fear of fat people. I apologize to the Californians—I just cut and pasted this one. I realize that it's referred to as "density challenged" in the "PC" state.

79. **Gerascophobia** – The fear of getting old. Two in a row? Come on!

80. **Chaetophobia** – The fear of hair. Bald men have lost this one.

81. **Nosocomephobia** – The fear of hospitals. Hello, that's where doctors keep the sick people.

82. **Ligyrophobia** – The fear of loud noises. And there it is, BAM!

83. **Didaskaleinophobia** – The fear of school. Uneducated people get this one.

84. **Technophobia** – The fear of technology. The most un-PC one of the bunch.

85. **Chronophobia** – The fear of the future. Because there was like, that movie—*The Day After Tomorrow*. And like, that Jake Gyllen-something guy was in it, and. . .

86. **Spheksophobia** – The fear of wasps. Seriously, it's the twenty-first century, people —you'd think we could get past all this racism!

87. **Ergophobia** – The fear of work. Only when a boss is involved.

88. **Darthophobia** — The fear of HARD work. (I slipped that one in while you were messing around reading this pointless list.)

89. **Coulrophobia** – The fear of clowns. Now what did I say above? Damn balloon-carryin' clowns. Makes me want to pop!

90. **Allodoxaphobia** – The fear of opinions. OMG, only other people's, right?

91. **Samhainophobia** – The fear of Halloween. They sugar-coated this one so much that I don't think it exists anymore.

92. **Photophobia** – The fear of light. People with Katsaridaphobia could use this one to their advantage.

93. **Disposophobia** – The fear of getting rid of stuff. I'm keeping this one . . . forever!

94. **Numerophobia** – The fear of numbers. Because they can get so BIG.

95. **Ombrophobia** – The fear of rain. [If the Wicked Witch of the West were played by Harrison Ford] Rain. . . Why does it always have to be rain?

96. **Coasterphobia** – The fear of roller coasters. Roller coasters, relationships—tomato, tom-ahto.

97. **Thalassophobia** – The fear of the ocean. Uh, hello again, that's where they keep the sharks.

98. **Scoleciphobia** – The fear of worms. This one is a whole can of trouble.

99. **Kinemortophobia** – The fear of zombies. I thought I was over this one and then that damned AMC released *The Walking Dead* and now it's back from the dead! Rotten people, just rotten!

100. **Myrmecophobia** – The fear of ants. This one's no picnic.

101. **Taphophobia** – The fear of being buried alive and waking up in a coffin. Back to *Kung Fu* obscure.

Whew! That was a seriously long list of fears.

Fear! Mongering, mutilating, mummifying fear! It gets in the way of damn near everything. And it's probably one of the biggest reasons potentially great authors delay their writing careers for years longer than they should've, yours truly included. We're simply afraid . . . of a lot of things.

But as big as that list of fears is, I know you'll agree that they left off the most important one for us budding writers.

AUTHORPHOBIA SUCKS

Authorphobia — the fear that your writing will suck. For writers and "aspiring" writers, it can be debilitating.

No BS, I looked it up on Google. Okay, I made it up, but it's as real as the book in your head that absolutely must get written.

And as someone who knows the fear and self-doubt involved in deciding to write your first novel, I can tell you that **authorphobia should've been number one**. I understand though, because in order to write that list . . . you'd have to first get over the fear that your fear list would suck. Which makes the fact that "authorphobia" didn't make it on the list . . . make more sense.

Special shout out to http://www.fearof.net for their fear list. And a helpful suggestion to make the list better—add authorphobia. It's a real sucking thing.

So **the world's full of fears**, real and imagined. And you've been exposed to them and reminded of the consequences for not heeding your fears, especiallythose telling you not to write. So . . . **what the heck can we do about that?**

SUPER SIMPLE SUCK BUSTER

COMMON WISDOM SUCKS!

Okay, I came across this suggestion out in the advice-o-sphere recently and I literally laughed out loud after reading it. Here goes: To conquer the fear that your writing will suck . . . wait for it. . .

Write down your fear . . . of sucking at writing.

Okay, now in reading that, it sounds like something where I would just touch off both barrels of a shotgun and pepper with a hefty dose of "you've got to be kidding me!"

You can just hear me now: "Let me get this straight. I have a fear of writing and you want me to . . . write that fear down?"

"Yes."

Okay, okay—I'll ease back a little, because it's actually not horrible advice. But on the surface. . . Wow!

Let's just go with it. Here I go:

"Okay, I am afraid to write . . . what I just wrote." Not so hard, but kinda silly-feeling too.

I'm just messing around, because that's not what that piece of advice really means. **We're not so much afraid to write**—we write all kinds of things down every day—**as we are afraid to *be writers*, to write what our hearts want us to write.**

Not blathering marketing material, not quarterly reports, not internal memos to the CEO that get us *Jerry McGuire* fired, but what we mean by "afraid to write" is afraid to write the things that matter to us most. Stories or poems or non-fiction books that we have painstakingly re-searched—**words we care about. Words from our soul.**

And then there's the criticism. . .

What we really *really* mean by "afraid to write" is that we're afraid what we write will be met with criticism, harsh and hurtful confidence-crushing criticism. That's what we really mean.

So, I guess the first step in that would be an alcoholic admission that we have a problem—we're afraid our writing will get criticized. **Because I don't even think the fear that we'll suck trumps the fear that someone else will tell us that we suck.**

What's next in that helpful, quick-and-dirty, fear-fixing, yet completely flummoxing advice?

THE WORST SUCK THAT CAN HAPPEN?

Ask your fearful little self **what's the worst thing that could happen** if you took a shot at writing a novel?

Uh, before I knew better, I could think of a lot of things. One of them being the only reality I knew of the publishing industry at the time—the ominous New York publishing house editor.

Self-doubt is the kissing cousin to fear.

I didn't submit my first effort at a fiction manuscript to a publishing house for one very real reason, in my mind anyway. That reason was that I knew it would get red-stamped with a New York publisher's huge stamp. One that they had to have specially made just for me, because, you know, I required a special kind of rejection that they'd never seen before. And that would require a customized stamp.

I imagined that stamp to read like this:

"Dear Mr. Windsor:

You suck.

In fact, from the looks of this manuscript, if you want to call this pile of excrement a "manuscript," you have always sucked. In all likelihood, you will suck henceforth and into eternity. Any children you have will most likely suck as well, thus continuing your sucky bloodline. I suggest you get a vasectomy to prevent passing on your sucky DNA.

You appear to have been knighted by the queen of suck. You could not suck more if you were a vampire.

Good day to you, Sir Suck—Count Suckula.

The "Editor" in charge of preventing suck

PS: Do not send any more of this suck to our offices."

That was the worst thing that I could imagine happening. And we both know it was totally, ludicrously unrealistic. There are good manuscripts and there are not-so-good manuscripts. And there are us rookies and there are those who have fought and battled and bled words for years. And at the time, my writing was not where it needed to be to get published and I knew that.

That's my story. I'm sticking to it.

But despite what you think, the universe wants you to write. Messengers come in all shapes. Start listening.

At the Peets coffeehouse where I do most of my suck—I mean writing—there was this guy. . . He was an interesting, suave dude, older than I was, and it was clear that he had no need to work because he was in the coffeehouse at all hours of the weekday.

Somehow we struck up a conversation about what I was doing, hunched over my laptop for twelve hours a day in a coffeehouse. I told him I was busy sucking at writing novels—in and of itself an insane leap of fearlessness—and he asked me where I was submitting all of my suck.

I started to go on about self-publishing and not submitting my manuscripts to publishing houses for fear of getting rejected. He just smiled at me.

La Femme Nikita? **That's like, my favorite. . .**

As it turned out, this guy had written and directed some episodes of the *La Femme Nikita* TV adaptation of the French movie turned U.S. blockbuster. He had also written some books, and his perspective on the entire thing threw my crazy fear of sucking for a loop.

"You aren't necessarily submitting your manuscript for

approval, because in all likelihood you will get rejected," he said. **"You have to think of it like you're opening up the first round of dialogue in negotiations that may last years.** And the twentieth time the same person hears or sees your name come across his or her desk, he or she may think, 'Hmmm, so and so seems serious.' "

The second thing he related to me, to my surprise, was that the same way I learned to write novels held true for learning to market them or submit them to a publisher.

You have to practice the steps and the format and the pitch letter to get better at it. **If you never submit once, you'll never get better at it.**

Even as I type it, I'm still flabbergasted at how utterly simple and right in front of my face his advice was.

I'm still afraid I'll suck.

Have I submitted a manuscript? Well, I still "chose" to go the self-publishing route, and I'd be lying if I told you that it wasn't because I was afraid of big-publisher criticism.

Fear . . . is irrational.

Fear is like that. It'll hold on tight and control you in the face of every rational and real bit of evidence that negates the very reason you're afraid.

Rationalizing with your fear is about as effective as re-reading the tired quote, "Fear is just False Expectations Appearing Real" in a motivational book for the umpteenth time.

CAN I HANDLE THE SUCK?

> *"You can't handle the truth!"* — **Jack Nicholson** in *A Few Good Men.* I love that line.

Step three in the super-simple suck-buster formula is to ask yourself if you **can handle that worst thing that could happen**. If your worst fear turned out to be true—you suck at writing—could you get over it?

Death, divorce, destruction, and dirty deeds done dirt cheap are all worse than some rejection that might bruise my ego, aren't they? So, rationally, my mind should be able to realize that I could handle a simple rejection letter, right?

Wrong. Still afraid.

Okay, so it's not gonna be as easy as some one-two-three blather about just looking irrational fear in the face and punching it. What then?

But before we get to that, **why the hell would you ever**

want to write anyway?

Maybe we should back up and see just how badly you want this.

WHY RISK SUCKING?

WHY DO YOU WANT TO SUCK?

"I write to make sense of my life." — John Cheever

Forget that no one can do this for you—**find the reason that finally convinces you beyond all fear to start writing**—but everyone's reason will be different. We're human beings after all—no two snowflakes alike and all that.

Oh sure, self-loathing is a national pastime, but you've done things before—started out at the bottom. **What makes writing any different** from a hundred other things that you may or may not have sucked at when you first started? Because once you started, you got better and with practice, eventually you got good.

I'll tell you point blank: **It's because writing matters to you.** You care about it. It's one thing to suck at something you couldn't care less about, quite another to suck at what you love.

But what will finally convince you that fear is not a good enough reason to delay your dream of writing any longer?

Here are a few suggestions to bust through your excuse-ridden reasons for not writing.

REASONS TO RISK SUCKING

Damn good reasons to write

Write because you've always wanted to. This is an easy one . . . seemingly. Yet for the scores of us who have always wanted to, but were still afraid, I'm sensing this one doesn't go deep enough into it.

Write because you have something to say. An interesting perspective, but if this were the case, you could keep a journal just as easily and "say" what you wanted to in that. No danger in a diary, right?

But that's not what you really want, is it?

Ahhh, now we're getting somewhere. **So, what we really want is for someone to "hear" what we have to "say."** A journal just isn't going to cut it. We're fiction storytellers —or non-fiction communicators—and we want to write novels, novellas or short stories for other people to read and enjoy.

We're getting closer.

Write because you might die today, or tomorrow, or next week. Leave something of yourself behind. Surely the fear of death would cure you? No? You sure? Because after you're gone it may be like you were never here. Might be nice for someone—your kids maybe—to read what it was like to be you or at least a story that spoke of you, don't you think?

Write because the fire inside of you will burn you alive if you don't. Now this one I like! I felt this for sure, and eventually this one will burn through the fear, but do you really want to wait thirty years for it to do that?

Write for yourself. But now we're back to journaling and that's not our problem. Write to be heard, understood and enjoyed, remember?

What about boredom? **We could write to cure boredom.** Not ours, but the world's.

> *"Boredom is a terminal problem. We have over-consumed, overstimulated and overindulged ourselves on this planet to the point of a blasé concern for its ruin. If you could cure boredom, you can save the world. And if you save the world... What better hero story is there than that?"* — **Anonymous** ... maybe... Okay, I said that.

Or if you don't like my take on it. . .

> *"We're past the age of heroes and hero kings. . . .*
> *Most of our lives are basically mundane and dull,*
> *and it's up to the writer to find ways to make them*
> *interesting."* — **John Updike** (He gets double
> bonus points for using that ellipsis between sen-
> tences for a dramatic pause.)

Write for someone else. This one's interesting. Maybe you're a hopeless romantic or maybe there's someone in your past that got away—the "one." That's a story that readers love and it makes money. Romance! Action! Drama! Those sell and in that order. So why not?

Write to get attention. Nothing wrong with liking attention. Actors, writers, rock stars, politicians and puppeteers have been doing things to get attention since each of them was invented. So, what's wrong with that?

Well, I'll tell you that the initial obscurity is going to squash that reason pretty quickly. **You'll have to write through "unknown" in order to get to the "fame and fortune,"** so the motivation behind this one may not last long.

And while we're on the subject of obscurity, realize that your fear of someone telling you that your writing sucks will be unfounded in the beginning. Obscurity will hide your suck for quite a while.

Comforting, I know.

SUCK FOR MONEY

That didn't sound right. . .

> *"Almost anyone can be an author; the business is to collect money and fame from this state of being."* — **A. A. Milne**

Write because you want to get rich. Nothing wrong with money—it motivates a heck of a lot of people to get even more done.

And that's the rub, right? Money. . . Hmmm, let's dig a little deeper into this one, because I see a lot of focus on money as a motivator to write and I think it's gotten a bad rap.

> *"Writing is turning one's worst moments into money."* — **J. P. Donleavy**

Think about that—if you could turn the worst things in your life on their heads? Take the poorest moments of your life and turn them into wealth generators? That would be something.

Remember, Darth Vader—*Hard work.*

"Writing is the only profession where no one considers you ridiculous if you earn no money." — **Jules Renard**

I'm not quite done with the money angle though, so let's hit it with a few more author quotes.

"No man but a blockhead ever wrote, except for money." — **Boswell**

Yeah. . . You know, it's been my experience that **the people who dole out the "helpful" advice of not being motivated by money** to pour their heart and soul into doing something, **usually give that advice after they've poured their heart and soul into something in order to acquire a lot of money**. Then, at the top of the mountain, they look back down into the valley and say to themselves, "Maybe I shouldn't have done this for the money."

But ask that same man or woman before the money—before they were rich. **The hindsight doesn't change the fact that many "successful" people got that way by going after the money.** And before this goes all altruistic assault on me, be honest: Who would you rather be, the Dalai Lama or Donald Trump?

Uh-huh, live on top of a cold mountain in a monastery? I

see all you little Donalds and Oprahs out there. You're not fooling anyone.

> *"I tire of reading pontificating advice from wealthy old men, advising against pursuing success at the motivation of money. This appears the purest of hypocrisies to me."* — **Steve Windsor**

And in coaching and writing and networking with new, intermediate and veteran authors in today's self-published landscape, **there's no more-talked-about, discussed, stressed, focused-on or fretted subject** at the forefront of the minds of writers, trying to write themselves out of a soul-sucking job . . . **than how to make more money**. "How to make money" books sell better than manuals on how to get laid.

However, there is this. . .

> *"The profession of book writing makes horse racing seem like a solid, stable business."* — **John Steinbeck**

Ouch.

But I got an even better reason for you to write. **Write . . . to get even.**

SWEET SUCKING REVENGE

> *"Revenge is sweet. Don't let anyone tell you different."* — **Steve Windsor** (Tweet this!)

So there I was—40,000 words of blathering banter between me and my alter-ego, super-me. Not commercially publishable and I didn't want that anyway. But what I *did* want was more of the awesome feeling that I got from writing. That was growing like an infection.

So I locked those words up—archived them on an external hard drive—and decided to write a "real" novel. Because even though my writing clearly sucked, it wasn't bad enough that it couldn't be fixed. Or so the forward momentum had me convinced.

But what to write about?

I was a burned-out, twenty-year Silicon Valley ex-IT director and I was *so* full of resentment for all I'd seen and participated in . . . and . . . and . . . and there it was!

I would write a novel about every micromanaging, moronic master I'd ever endured . . . and at the end . . . I'd kill them all! Perfect.

ROOKIE SUCK BUSTER:

They say that this is rookie mistake #1—believing that

your own story is a good story. However, I was a rookie, so I didn't care. More accurately, I didn't know any better.

Anyway, as far as that goes, I said it in my *Nine Day Novel: Outlining* book: **If writing about your own journey overcomes the fear and gets the draft of your first novel done, just do it**. You need the practice, trust me.

Let me give you a hint—you'll love doing this. So off I went.

But being who I am, I made another rookie mistake: I set out to write not one sucking novel but a trilogy of them so monumentally sucky that they turned into a four-part sucking epic!

And the fear? Where did the fear go?

I'll let you in on another little secret: If you're willing to just trust me—**forward motion will crush fear and leave it crying and bloody in an alley**.

Get moving.

Just start typing your thoughts if you're stuck. Pretty soon those thoughts can't help flowing into a reasonable direction. Some people call it mind-mapping. I call it visual vomit—spewing everything onto a page or notepad until themes take shape. I won't go into detail. Google it and see if you think it'll work for you.

Careful though—fear is resilient, so it never really dies. It may go dormant, but it won't be far off. It'll just limp along behind you, like a zombie that wants to eat you alive if you let it catch up. The trick is to keep moving . . . and not to trip.

All of that too greedy?

Too petty? Too bourgeois for you? Pumping prose for profit not in your . . . personality? No pent-up anger to exercise? No lost love to lament?

Okay, let's switch gears.

ANSWERING THE CALL TO SUCK

Is writing the only thing you've ever wanted to do in your entire life? **Were you born to write?**

Or maybe you just decided this morning that you want to write a novel.

Quick, get a notepad out and write down the first thing that comes into your mind. I'm serious.

Even if it's "This Steve Windsor author guy is an annoying, arrogant ass and I don't like him. I really need to find another writing mentor to follow and read and learn from, because this Darth Vader persona crap is grinding on my nerves and . . . and I bet his novels *do* suck! I'm never reading them. In fact, I'm gonna go leave him a bad review without even reading the book! And—"

And therein lies a powerful method to teach yourself to start writing.

SLY SUCK BUSTER:

Ten things I hate

The "10 Things I Hate" fighting your way through the fear and blockage to write totally awesome, sneaky suck buster. Here's what I want you to do:

Get out your laptop or a piece of paper and pencil—I don't care what you use—and then you're going to **write down ten things that you really hate.** Just list them out. Don't tell me you don't have them. Start with taxes if you have to. That one's easy.

And the first thing I want you to do is **rip your "nice" filter off**, because it has no place in this exercise. If you're typically known as the "nice" one, I want you to get extra mean about all those hidden things you never, ever speak up and say to anyone. I know you got 'em, lurking there behind all that nice.

Pick things you really loathe and write about them in the most vile and vicious way you can. Don't edit, don't temper, just write the terrible truth. Write a paragraph for each one. Go!

You back? Did you do it? Seriously, go do it or I'll give you a reason to. . .

You're back. Great! Now, read that exercise back to yourself . . . out loud.

You just puckered, didn't you?

I did this with one of my coaching students recently, and whereas before she was completely stumped as to what and how to start writing, twenty minutes later she'd written such eloquent and descriptive venom that I pretty much **dispelled her belief that she "sucked at writing."**

As she read back her own words, she didn't recognize the voice as her own. Yet it was hers . . . and it was beautifully written.

Connect with the anger.

Often we don't realize how emotionally available our feelings of anger are to us. While we can barely articulate what we truly love, we are absolutely crystal-chandelier clear about what we hate.

If you didn't do the exercise, go back and try it. You'd be surprised. And remember—don't filter.

If you haven't guessed by now, I'm kind of tricking you. Here's what I mean.

ALL WRITERS SUCK

ALL WRITERS SUCKED

At one time or another . . . every author sucked. So, to a certain extent, deciding to write is by definition planning to suck . . . at first.

And once you do that, you'll join the ranks of professional sucking authors everywhere. But don't let anyone tell you you're not a great writer.

Who's to say what "great" writing is, anyway? If you write a letter to your grandmother, you're a great writer. If you write a thank-you card to a friend, you're a great writer.

Uh-oh, I feel a Jeff Foxworthy "you might be a redneck" segue coming.

You might be a great writer. . .

- If you write ten words a day . . . you might be a great writer.
- If you write a thousand words every morning . . . you might be a great writer.
- If you write resumes for the unemployment

office all day . . . you might be a great writer.

- If you find yourself musing after you read a novel that you could do that . . . you might be a great writer.

- If you find spelling, grammar and sentence structure errors in anything you read . . . you might be a great writer.

- If you love stories and have a million of them in your head . . . you might be a great writer.

- If you have notebooks upon notebooks—or even just a few—of poems, half-finished stories and one-liner observations that you won't let anyone read . . . you are most certainly a great writer.

Being a great writer is about you writing. And at first that writing will suck. **Get over it. We all sucked when we first started.**

The value of your writing isn't what some professor says it is. And it isn't what the New York Times Bestseller list says it is. It's not J.K. Rowling or Stephen King or a bunch of dead people from the eighteenth century. It's not even what some reviewer on Amazon says it is either.

Let's get clear—writing is simply communicating.

Writing is a method of communication that's been

around since cavemen figured out how to use chunks of burned wood to scrawl black soot on the walls of their caves. And you can bet your ass that there wasn't a critic standing behind that first caveman or woman saying, "Zogina, that not look like ox. That not even look like pig. You suck at cave scrawling, Zogina. Suck bad."

Do you know why? Because not only did Zogina not care, but in all likelihood she turned around and clubbed that chirping chatterer over the head with what was left of her half-burned scrawling stick. And then she went back to drawing her "ox." Only then, instead of having one color— black soot—she had a little bit of crimson red to work with to depict the hunt for the ox.

Don't listen to people who peddle a pompous notion of what it means to be an author—write anything you want, if you want to be a writer. Don't buy into the idea that you're only an author if you live in New York and are on the NYT bestseller list. **There's no "real" writing; there's just writing** and to do it all you need to do is . . . write.

- Write because you're mad that you let the fear of sucking stop you from writing earlier.
- Write because you're so happy that you're finally going to write.
- Write because you love someone and they don't love you back.

- Write because they do love you back.

- Write to feel, to learn, to love, and to laugh.

- Write because you don't even need a reason.

- Write through your frustration and fear and failure, if that's where you are.

- Write because you're lost and you need to "find" yourself. (Writing will definitely help you do that!)

"Writing became an outlet for my dissatisfaction, distaste, and my way of trying to make sense of what was happening around me. It was my way to explore personally what I didn't understand." — **Terry McMillan**

Write because no one else can or ever will be able to write like you. Tell your story your way.

And write . . . because it's the only way to get better at it.

WRITING'S THE BEST SUCKING JOB

YOU CAN SUCK NAKED

> *"It's perfectly acceptable to write while you're naked. Even when you're safely inside your own home."* — **Steve Windsor** (Tweet this!)

Forget that **you have the freedom to write from anywhere, anytime and about anything you want**, you don't have to get dressed up to do it. You don't have to get dressed at all if you don't want to. In fact, many days I don't even get out of bed—I reach over to my desk, grab my laptop, flip it open and start writing. Never mind how cool that is, think of the efficiency.

> *"My main reason for adopting literature as a profession was that, as the author is never seen by his clients, he need not dress respectably."* — **George Bernard Shaw**

You're gonna save the planet by writing.

I spent twenty years in high-technology startups in Silicon Valley, commuting back and forth on jammed freeways, so thick with coffee-guzzling zombies that it seemed a miracle anyone ever made it to work at all.

My typical commute was one hour each way. Many times, if some poor unfortunate motorist glanced down at his or her watch at the wrong moment and ended up in a fender bender, that hour turned to an hour and a half each way. Or worse, an injury accident would bring the entire rushing mess of us lemmings to a grinding halt.

If you figure that at a minimum of two hours a day for fifty weeks a year (subtract the two weeks they let you recover in the ICU from the suck of your job) times five days a week, that's 500 hours a year—25% of a full-time job . . . completely wasted behind the wheel of a car! I can guarantee you that it was closer to 750 hours—almost a half-time job!

Project that out to the number of people doing that each day and figure out what the equivalent loss in GNP productivity would be for a nation of zombified commuters. Insane!

Think of how much writing I could have been doing.

Save the planet—become a writer. A new bumper sticker, maybe?

THE FREEDOM TO SUCK

Writing for a living is the closest thing to freedom you'll ever taste. No bosses, no deadlines (kinda). . .

> *"The big motivation for me was the desire to be independent, to get up when you want, write what you want, and work where you want."* — **Irving Wallace**

With great freedom comes great responsibility.

If freedom is the ability to do what you truly want when you want, then it's also the *obligation* to do that as well. There will be no one to stand over your shoulder like a boss, micromanaging your efforts to get your work done. For that matter, **there will be no "done"—no finish line.**

There will simply be the next thing you need to write, the next read-through or the next technique to learn. The next beautiful piece of suck to send into the stratosphere. And you'll be free to do that as you feel the need.

And then . . . there's that whole "writing in a cool coffee-house" thing. For me, that alone is worth blasting through the fear.

> *"The idea of just wandering off to a cafe with a notebook and writing and seeing where that takes me for a while is just bliss."* — **J. K. Rowling**

And yet, there's still that fear . . . and the self-doubt . . . and the excuses.

Let's go take a look at some more of those excuses. Come on. . . *Bring* your suck with you.

IT'S NEVER TOO LATE TO SUCK

I'M TOO OLD TO SUCK

"How vain it is to sit down to write when you have not stood up to live." — **Henry David Thoreau**

Pushing 49 at the publication of this, my eighth commercial book, this excuse is near and dear to my heart. Oh how I wish I would've started thirty years ago. Think of what I could've. . . Uh, yeah. . . That's not reality.

The writing I do now, and the writing you'll do at any point in your life, will be influenced by the cumulation of all the events of your life. Were you to have never lived that life, your writing from that experience wouldn't be possible.

"All writing is cremated youth." — **Willa Cather**

Think about it: If you had never lived life in the way you had, could you write about it with the authority that you most certainly will?

How to write about love and loss and lust without ever having experienced those emotions? Or to write about old age or regret without knowing those feelings? Or the happiness of seeing a friend that you thought you'd lost years ago? Or the deep love and affection you have for someone, having gone through the trials, tribulations and triumphs of life, side by side with them?

Could a twenty-year-old write *The Bridges of Madison County*? Maybe, but probably not with the perspective of Robert James Waller. That would take a lot of research and an author still might miss the nuance that the actual experience, or the emotions of a similar experience, would give them.

Thankfully, there's simply no date stamp on your career as a writer.

SUCK BUSTER:

To give you a little perspective on it, read this book. It's one of my favorites:

Barbara Sher - *It's Only Too Late If You Don't Start Now: How to Create Your Second Life At Any Age*

Barbara is considered the fairy godmother of life coaching and has written several self-help books that focus on going after your dreams no matter your age or situation. Seriously, if you feel like "my train has left the station," "my ship has sailed" or "I'm just too old for this shit," read her book. You'll change your mind.

QUOTES FROM SOME OLD SUCKERS

Here are just a few of the authors who didn't start sucking until after they turned 40.

Anthony Burgess, 40 — He's most famous for *A Clockwork Orange*, which came out when he was 45.

Bram Stoker, 50 — *Dracula*.

Laura Ingalls Wilder, 65 — She didn't start writing until after she retired. Her first book, *Little House in the Big Woods*, came out in 1932, and kicked off her *Little House* series. *Little House on the Prairie* came out in 1935 and spawned a TV series of the same name.

Alex Haley was 55 when *Roots* came out.

Watership Down was written by **Richard Adams** when he was 52. If you have no idea what book that is, you may have missed high school. It came out in 1972 though, so. . .

If none of this talk of experience and age strikes a chord with you, chances are you're too young to empathize with it. Luckily, you need only live and wait and you'll be informed soon enough.

In the meantime, let's take a look at what you might be feeling as *resistance* instead.

IT'S NEVER TOO EARLY TO SUCK

I'M TOO YOUNG TO SUCK

> *"Most of the basic material a writer works with is acquired before the age of fifteen."* — **Willa Cather**

Here's another quote:

> *"Youth is wasted on the young."* — **George Bernard Shaw**

It doesn't really mean what most people think it means. We "older" citizens remember what it was like to be young. We loved and hoped and remained optimistic about anything and everything. We threw ourselves into new things and new situations with reckless abandon. We could party and abuse our bodies, and run marathons the next day and then rinse and repeat the entire thing the next night.

When you're young, hangovers are shorter, erections are longer and you only dye your hair to have a cool new color, not to cover up gray. The wild flashes of your life aren't the "hot" kind. And your body? Let's just say, all things defy gravity when you're young.

Sucking when you're young, especially at writing? Well, why not do it then?

In fact, when you're young, you spend remarkably little time, compared to us grizzled life vets, worrying about whether you'll be any good at something. Mistakes are just glitches and recovering from them is a certainty. You can use that to your advantage. Suck early and often . . . at writing, I say.

What that quote above really means is that most of us who've aged beyond those early years realize how wonderful they were and how much opportunity we had to live in the moment, free from worry and strife of spent and possibly misspent youth.

I do realize that's not everyone's experience, but for many of us, it was.

My advice? Write it all down. Keep a journal, hide a diary, write poems. . . Trust me, one day you'll wish you had.

> *"Oh, how we should have penned more poems, written more romance—more lines of lust and love."* — **Steve Windsor** (Tweet this!)

And the best news of all about starting to write while you're young. . .

There's no entrance exam to start writing—anyone can do it. No rite of passage that you must first go through. Anyone at any age and any skill level can decide that they want to write and then . . . simply start writing. And if you're willing to do the same hard work, practice and research that everyone else has to, no matter your age, you can and will start sucking less and less each day. And who knows, maybe you'll even get rich and famous.

Real authors simply start writing down the suck . . . no matter their age.

So keep your journal, write in your diary. Write sucky poems about love and cry on the paper or keyboard. Or write about the monsters under your bed and how you can hear them plotting to take over the world. Write about how no one will listen to you and you're the only one who can save the future from those monsters. Because . . . you really are.

As a double whammy, I'm about to make you feel so embarrassed for being fearful about starting to write, that you'll probably go out and pen your first novel tomorrow.

Two words—Helen Keller

At nineteen months, Helen Keller got sick and became deaf and blind. Shortly before Keller's seventh birthday, Anne Sullivan arrived to serve as her instructor. At age eleven, Keller wrote a short story, "The Frost King," that she sent as a gift to the head of the Perkins School for the Blind. The story was published in the school's magazine.

Forget that a deaf and blind girl wrote a story, here's what happened next. . .

Helen Keller was accused of plagiarism! Her story was said to be too close to Margaret Canby's "Frost Fairies." And then they had a trial. Keller "won," but had a nervous breakdown as a result of the stress. Then, at twenty-two, she published her autobiography, *The Story of My Life.*

Let me recap that for you: **Deaf and blind, got a tutor, learned to write, wrote a short story, got accused of plagiarism, nervous breakdown, wrote the story of her life.**

When I read that, I was like, "I suck, and I need to write more."

The suck still got you limp? It's okay. It happens to a lot of authors. It's nothing to be ashamed of.

What's next? What hurdle do we need to jump over to get you writing?

YOU'RE SO SUCKING WORTHY

WE'RE NOT SUCKING WORTHY

That isn't a *Wayne's World* basement cable show slogan, rolling around in your head. It's actually one of the most common fears all authors at all stages of their careers suffer from.

> *"Comparison is the enemy to creativity."* — **E'yen A. Gardner**

Chances are, if you long to write, you're a little on the sensitive side of the spectrum. You're probably, though not certainly, a little "touchy-feely."

Most of the time, that's a good thing—the ability to understand what others feel and describe complex emotions you may or may not have experienced as you write your stories.

As a creative writer that trait will serve you well. But sometimes all that empathy will turn on you like a family pit bull going berserk at a third-grader's birthday barbecue.

Mind the pit bull, love.

Then, frozen in fear, you'll watch as whatever creative confidence you've been able to muster will get ripped apart in the jaws of self-doubt and inadequacy.

The only solace you'll have in that bloodbath? **You're definitely not alone**—there are authors and writers all around you, screaming the same thing: "The suck mutt's got me! The suck mutt's got me!"

Even long-time successful authors constantly compare themselves to other authors. But let's dig a little deeper into what those feelings are really all about.

We live in a comparison culture.

In our ever-connected technological world, we're bombarded daily by millionaires, billionaires and Beverly Hills benefactors to the point that we've acquired the completely false belief that everyone's rich and successful. And furthermore, they had to do seemingly very little work to get there.

And then we learn to believe that in comparison, our lives simply suck.

This goes double for writers.

For writers, and especially if you had to endure a creative literature class, iconic "gods" are held up in front of you like pillars of the unattainable. Their books are placed on pedestals to remind you of how "inadequate" and pointless your own writing will inevitably be. Kafka, George Bernard Shaw, Longfellow, Anne Rice, Virginia Woolf. . . How the hell will you ever measure up to them?

Even in the research for this book, monolithic figures were seemingly the only place to find the wisdom and motivation to understand writing and the writing life. I wondered how we mortals could do this godly work. It must be . . . next to impossible.

And don't even get me started on Stephen King envy.

It seems like everyone with a writing pulse will hold up anything that Stephen King says as gospel. Love the books, but it's just as valid for you to tell *yourself* how to write as it is to listen to someone saying, "Stephen King says only to write on Thursdays, so I only write on Thursdays."

Uh, hello, how am I going to finish my novel in nine days if I can only write on Thursdays?

Sarcasm aside, **comparing yourself to other writers is like a single raindrop comparing itself to a flood**. We're all part of the creative consciousness of humanity and we all have a light to shine that is unique and—oh, dammit! I hate it when my inner-writer goes all creative muse mushery on me.

The bottom line is that comparison is pointless.

You're you—there is no other "suck" like your writing. You will never be able to write that Stephen King "suck" or J.K. Rowling's "suck," let alone all that "suck" in E. L. James' suckfest (that's a . . . pun), or that Franz Kafka suck. But chances are high, **if you do the hard work and improve yourself, practice your writing, your writing will suck less than it did yesterday**—suck less tomorrow than it did today. That's what you should strive for—sucking less every day.

And there's simply no way to do that—get that improvement—unless you write.

> *"Always dream and shoot higher than you know you can do—try to be better than yourself."* —
> **John Steinbeck**

Do the best you can today and realize that even the almighty King was once a self-critical yearner just like you . . . until his wife pulled that *Carrie* story that everyone told him "sucked" out of the garbage—so the story goes—and the rest of it was hard work, hustle and history.

"If you have an old habit of competing and comparing yourself with others, then you're still living your life like a sperm. GROW UP!" — **Saurabh Sharma**

Writing, writing and more writing. That's how you become an author.

No other profession is as simple in its execution. And there's no other path to greatness clearer than to continually improve your writing. Only way to do that is to stop comparing yourself to others and start comparing today's words with yesterday's.

If your writing's getting better, you are most certainly worthy.

THERE'S PLENTY OF SUCKING TIME

WRITING IS A TIME SUCK

Here's a little acronym I came up with as it relates to writing:

T.I.M.E.

Time Invested Means Everything.

Whatever you believe about writing, to get better, you'll have to carve out time. I'm not gonna deep-dive on this, because I did a brutal and exhaustive recount of my often-misunderstood time tactics in *Nine Day Novel: Writing*.

Suffice to say, you gotta put in the hours if you want your writing to get better. There are a million excuses why you don't have enough time, but every one of them is just fear manifesting itself as failure to write.

Do the math.

If a "commercial" novel is 90,000 words—I've done that

math, too—then you can use math to help you through the fear.

Once you get into the zone, immersed in writing, you will probably be able to type around 1,000 words per hour. At that pace, a 90k novel will take you 90 hours to complete your first sucky draft.

Unless you type faster—improve your word count—that draft wants 90 hours of your life. Figure out where you're going to get those hours . . . or stop pretending you're going to write a novel.

THE SIMPLEST SUCK BUSTER I KNOW:

Shut off your TV during the entire time you're writing that draft. There, you now have a national average of four hours a day to dedicate to your novel.

Congratulations, you'll be done in 22.5 days.

TALENT SUCKS

TALENT TROLLS SUCK

Listen, **a lack of talent isn't stopping many writers from becoming successful authors.** Trust me on that one. You wouldn't believe some of the suck that sells. Even my suck sells okay. LOL

> *"It took me fifteen years to discover that I had no talent for writing, but I couldn't give it up because by that time I was too famous."* — **Robert Benchley**

Assessing talent is as subjective as critically reviewing a novel.

That cuts at the very core of this fear. Saying someone is good at something or not good at it, especially a creative endeavor like writing or painting or composing music. . .

Cliche as it sounds, beauty truly is in the eye of the beholder. And oftentimes the beauty of something "changes" as more and more people discover it.

Following the herd . . . sucks for real.

If you had no historical context or were never told that Leonardo da Vinci's *Mona Lisa* is one of the finest paintings ever created, you might see it for the first time and say, "I don't like that. She's not even smiling. Da Vinci had no talent." But inside the context of "everyone" agreeing that it's a masterpiece. . .

> *"A wildebeest will follow the herd right into the jaws of the crocodiles. I'd rather be a crocodile."* —
> **Steve Windsor** (Tweet this!)

There's an argumentation theory called argumentum ad populum (Latin for "appeals to the people"). **It's an argument that concludes that something is true because many people believe it:** "If many believe so, it is so."

It's my theory that **this applies to authors and fiction novels rather well.**

Many serious fiction critics consider Charles Dickens to be one of the classic writers. However, in his time he was the equivalent of a comic book serial writer, releasing almost all of his work as a series of stories whose plots were not even outlined or finished until he wrote the final chapters.

Even E.L. James struggled to get her famous hanky-panky, spanky-spanky books into readers' hands. In the end (Not a pun. Okay, maybe), the "stinging" popularity of her books happened because the global herd of housewives got hold of them and told everyone they knew that the books were . . . titillating. Not that they weren't, but that's the way popularity takes over.

The hindsight to assess greatness is astounding, as is the forethought to determine that a work is worthless before it has even endured the time it takes for its author to die.

In truth, many great authors only became that way after their deaths, while struggling endlessly during their lives.

We'll talk about that in the next chapter.

MAD SUCKING SKILLS

Skills trump talent.

So, once again, we're back to hard work. Funny how that keeps popping up.

There's no shortage of feedback from critics, literary professors, journalists—you name it—who say writing can only be done by the talented. Everyone else has to be satisfied with sucking. **But what is talent other than skills, practiced relentlessly?**

Take a look at what the "Fresh Prince of Bel Air" has to say about the subject.

> *"Talent . . . you have naturally. Skill is only developed by hours and hours and hours of beating on your craft."* — **Will Smith**

Not comfortable following the advice of an actor who calls himself "not especially talented," but instead relied on a "sick work ethic" to rise to the top of his profession? Still afraid you'll never be able to learn to "fly"?

Okay, here's the wildly successful author of—pun intended—*Fear of Flying* to help convince you:

> *"Everyone has talent. What is rare is the courage to follow the talent to the dark places where it leads."* — **Erica Jong**

If you feel like you have no talent, or even if you feel completely gifted, I'll let you in on a little secret—**it doesn't matter**.

What does matter is your willingness to learn and work hard by writing more, better, and eventually, faster.

SUCK BUSTER:

"Planning to write is not writing. Outlining . . . researching . . . talking to people about what you're doing, none of that is writing. Writing is writing."
E.L. Doctorow

Suck it up and write! Just write, baby. Just write. . .

I'm serious. Get out your computer, laptop, notepad—whatever—and simply write everything that pops into your head for five minutes. Put a timer on and do it. Write blather. Go!

No ideas? Okay, I'll help you start. Finish this:

A rabbit, a reverend and a rhino walk into a symphony. And the rhino says to the reverend. . .

UPDATE: a favorite fan of mine gave me the punchline to this joke. "The Rhino says, 'I hope they have a horn section.' "

Yep! Just make stuff up. After all, what is fiction writing if it's not total immersed imagination?

Two things will happen if you do this exercise: You'll stop worrying about what you put down, what you write will get better as you go . . . and at the end of the five minutes, you'll want more time. Okay, three things.

I almost went off on a rant. Thankfully, I'll stop myself and "crutch" back on some quotes.

> *"I write to give myself strength. I write to be the characters that I am not. I write to explore all the things I'm afraid of. "* — **Joss Whedon**

Hey, did you notice that? As we write—as this book progresses—we're starting to see a lot less suck. That only happens when you write.

> *"Do the thing you fear and the death of fear is certain."* — **Ralph Waldo Emerson**

LITERARY LIFE AFTER DEATH SUCKS

FAME AND FORTUNE CAN SUCK

Do you long to be a rich and famous author? Be careful with that.

The fact is, many struggling authors didn't become rich and famous until after they were dead. But does that mean you shouldn't try to do it or that those authors lacked the talent we were just talking about?

Does it mean that suddenly, upon their deaths, a magical talent fairy descended from the heavens and bestowed magnificence on their writing? Hardly.

Most of them worked their asses off during their lives. And the books they published didn't change significantly from when they published them to when they became "classics," making those men and women famous and posthumously wealthy.

The writings remained powerful works of art from the time they were written to the time they were accepted as "fact." What changed was perspective, popularity and people's awareness of them.

During their lives the public thought they sucked, and after they died, they didn't suck? Hmmmm. . .

Who knows, **you could be the next [insert famous dead author's name here]** whose works are crammed down the throats of creative literature students, gushing that they'll never be able to write seriously until they can write like you do.

And then your heirs will bask in the fortunes that your novels create for them, while you slumber soundly, peacefully, six feet under the ground. Doesn't that sound tragically Shakespearian? Uh, a little sucky, if you ask me.

In some cases literary "success" isn't all it's cracked up to be.

In fact, what we want—at least this is what I'm after—is to create some wealth and maybe even a little notoriety long before our novels are discovered in the dusty attic by our second cousin's third niece's granddaughter, because we were too afraid to publish and promote them during our own lifetimes.

First, so we can get rid of some of that successful author envy, here are a few authors who, despite their best efforts, left legacies behind instead of living lavish lives:

Plato

There was no notoriety in Plato's time—no widespread fame and fortune. **He wrote because he loved it and he had something to say.** Only hundreds of years later did his ideas and writings gain international fame for their political and social insight.

Anne Frank

Not only was Anne Frank's life tragic, but her death left behind one of the best known, widely read and heartfelt works of art there ever was. Not the best way to become literarily famous. *The Diary of Anne Frank*.

Franz Kafka

I can tell you that having to read *The Metamorphosis* in college truly sucked. "Fantastic work of literary fiction" is a subjective term indeed. Kafka wasn't famous during his life, but there's hardly a college literature professor alive who allowed his or her students to escape reading about Gregor Samsa waking up as a bug.

As a side note, Kafka is another story of what almost wasn't. He asked a friend to burn his manuscripts when he died. Friends being what they are, even after death, Kafka's dying wish was ignored and millions of college students still mourn over his legacy, tortured each semester by sadistic professors assigning Kafka as required reading.

This one's for all the environmentalists out there:

Henry David Thoreau

This guy lived in the woods, pondering the benefits of being a hermit. He wasn't widely known in his life. Far ahead of his time and the future disciples of the prevention of environmental destruction, his appreciation of the outdoors, social activism, and writings on nature weren't wildly embraced by the public of his time.

Oh, and guess what? Thoreau couldn't find a publisher for many of his books, so in a few cases he used his own money—can you imagine—to publish. Sadly, there was no digital or on-demand publishing in Thoreau's time. He sold very few of the books he printed . . . which I'm sure must have sucked.

Emily Dickinson

Dickinson, for all intents and purposes, was a recluse. It was only after her death that her family found almost 1,800 poems of Emily's—most of her writings. And thus her legacy was born . . . after she died.

There's a hidden lesson in Emily Dickinson as well, and that was that she didn't really seem to care about the fame or the money. **What she loved was the writing** and she definitely did the hard work.

Several-hundred-year-deceased writers is one thing, but we may be in danger of doing what our college professors do in holding up demigods for us to compare ourselves to —showing us how badly we suck.

Someone. . . A slightly more contemporary author, maybe?

Stieg Larsson

I know, right. Who? You may better recognize him as the author of *The Girl With the Dragon Tattoo*. The best-selling book in the U.S. in 2010, adapted into a blockbuster Hollywood movie. Poor Stieg—dead before he could enjoy the spoils of stardom.

Here comes the poster child for the author struggling in anonymity only to become famous after death. The master of the macabre. . .

Edgar Allen Poe

Poe is famous for living in poverty and dying the same way, though he desperately craved fame and recognition. He finally got it . . . after they found him dead in an alley at the age of 40. Now his works are the precursor to the classic bullet-ridden bloodfests that Hollywood adores.

Herman Melville

Melville desperately wanted to succeed. Sound familiar? He had some success writing about sea adventures. So he started a little book called *Moby Dick*.

Leave out that we wouldn't have Starbucks coffeehouses without it, but *Moby Dick* was supposed to be a nice average-length novel about an obsessed Captain Ahab hunting a whale. But the book got away from Melville and turned into the gigantic paperweight we know today.

Not that anyone who's read it really feels any differently, but readers at the time hated *Moby Dick*. Critics followed that "herd" rule I mentioned earlier and ripped it to shreds in reviews. An enduring age-old tradition, it seems.

Moby Dick "sunk" Melville. Then that cliche author boozin' took him and that was that.

After his death, Melville's fame was buried only to be dug up in the 1920s. Even if you've never read it, chances are high you've heard of it. *Moby Dick* survives Melville's death as an immortal classic.

Had enough? Ready to start writing yet? No? No worries —we're just getting started.

Let's see what we can do about curing the fear, getting you writing, and making sure someone reads your books . . . before you're dead, shall we?

Here's a final word from another author long gone but

never forgotten:

> *"I was sorry to hear my name mentioned as one of the great authors, because they have a sad habit of dying off. Chaucer is dead, so is Milton, so is Shakespeare, and I am not feeling very well myself."* — **Mark Twain**

MY FIRST NOVEL SUCKED

THERE I WAS, SUCKING. . .

"You don't start out writing good stuff. You start out writing crap and thinking it's good stuff, and then gradually you get better at it. That's why I say one of the most valuable traits is persistence." — **Octavia Butler**

Back to my own little special snowflake author saga.

There I was—40,000 words of non-commercial suck under my belt and feeling pretty good about myself. Nothing like word count to boost your confidence.

I'd researched and studied and learned and written like a rabid dog at a mouth-foaming festival. What next?

Time for a "real" novel, I reasoned. Or maybe an epic three-part—no, four-part—series! Yep, let's get 'er done. By then I was starting to get the feeling that—could it be? —I was a writer. The fear was giving way to forward motion and action. The more I wrote, the less fear I felt.

"In the action is the power." — **Steve Windsor**

(Tweet this!)

So I hit the coffeehouse with a vengeance and over the course of about three months, I wrote around 240,000 words of the first draft of the first novel in that series. How?

Simply put, I didn't waste a lot of time asking myself or anyone else if I was allowed to practice writing fiction—suck at it—I just did it because I knew it was the only way to get better. I'd proven to myself, with my little journal disguised as a fiction tale, that I could put down words. Now, I just had to herd them all to the crocodiles.

I threw myself into the beauty of words flowing from my fingertips, and in that action—the writing, re-searching, reading, ranting onto the page—there was no room or time for doubt. If I got stuck, I researched and read and revised and kept going. If I was unsure, I blazed past that doubt and fear to the next thing—the next line or page or chapter.

> *"Writing's no different from anything else—the doing crowds out the doubt."* — **Steve Windsor**
> (Tweet this!)

I was sucking less and less each day.

Was that novel my big hit? Hardly. As of the writing of this book, that first novel, named *Cramdown,* sits on my Cre-ateSpace and Kindle dashboards, unpublished, in need of a serious re-edit and word count trim. (Even though I edited it down to 140,000 words.)

Pointless, say you. Perfect, say I. (How the hell did *pi-rates* get in here? Darth. . .)

I needed the practice.

You wouldn't believe how much you learn by writing a Four Part Story Structure plotted with roughly twenty characters in five different countries, doing the research and creating avatars for each character and. . . It was both maddening and fascinating and educational all at the same time. No college course taught me as much.

Yes, my first "real" novel sucked and still sucks today. I wouldn't have it any other way.

Without that book, I couldn't have written the next one in the series even better. And then half-finished the next one in that series. But then I wrote four more novels that were much better, and then I wrote these non-fiction books, and then. . .

Without that first completely mistake-laden, verbose, adverb-riddled pile of rookie author cliches and punctua-tion mistakes, it's quite possible that none of it would've ever happened and I wouldn't be writing this book.

I love that first novel, and presently I'm working on cleaning it up to republish it, because in it there's a story buried that I know a fan is waiting for.

SUCK BUSTER:

Write your first novel, let it suck, learn, and then move on . . . and write another.

After all, practice will save democracy. Take a look. . .

> *"Reading and writing, like everything else, improve with practice. And, of course, if there are no young readers and writers, there will shortly be no older ones. Literacy will be dead, and democracy—which many believe goes hand in hand with it—will be dead as well."* — **Margaret Atwood**

You see, you're toying with the entire free world by not beginning your writing career right now.

Don't let a little thing like fear stop you from saving democracy!

IT TAKES A SUCKING VILLAGE

NEVER SUCK ALONE

Here's as good a place as any to revisit the "rules" of writing. Most author advice will tell you to stay away from politics and profanity. Most of the time, I say "suck" that!

However, I made one big mistake writing my first book and then my first two and a half novels. Beyond the profanity and the politics, that is. Can you figure out what it was? No?

I tried to do it all on my own.

You don't have to do this alone.

I coach a lot of first-time, hopeful, yet sometimes scared shitless writers who want to either finally learn how to write and publish their first novel or republish one that's languishing in obscurity.

To a person, each one of them struggles with the same feelings of fear and inadequacy. **Most of them absolutely believe that their dream to write is stupid, crazy or naive.** And almost to a person . . . **they believe that**

they're alone in that feeling. But inside a community of other first-time authors, something wonderful happens. They each find that they aren't unique snowflakes of fear after all.

And once they realize that their self-doubt was a shared feeling that every new author gets just before they commit to letting go and doing the hard work, they each marvel at how easily those fears are left behind and overcome.

Surrounded by people who completely understand their struggles—all solving the problems any new author faces—it's easier to wade through the suck to get to the success.

Once the focus is off of self-doubt, self-loathing, and self-pity, they're free to concentrate on the tactics and hard work that will get their novels and books not only published, but surprisingly to them, popular.

Community grows confidence.

SUCK BUSTER:

Find a community to share your author journey with. One of the best places for author communities is Facebook. There are several good groups. Search for writers, authors or Kindle publishers as a start.

Don't join every one of them; just find a couple you like and then follow and participate and you'll learn a ton. One of the best ones is **Pat Flynn's First Kindle Book**. And Lise Cartwright and I run the Author Basics Facebook Group of aspiring authors.

And remember this. . .

> *"Writing is a lonely job, unless you're a drinker, in which case you always have a friend within reach."*
> — **Emilio Estevez** (Thought I forgot about that Emilio quote, didn't you?)

WRITING IS SUCKING FUNNY

HAVE SOME SUCKING FUN

> *"A pen is certainly an excellent instrument, to fix a man's attention and to inflame his ambition."* — **John Adams** in his autobiography

If you can't see the absolute gem of an opportunity for irreverent humor in that above quote, let me help you out. I like to poke fun at . . . pretty much everything, so apologies in advance if I offend you.

I'll give you a hint—I think Adams mistakenly put a character space in there.

> *"A penis is certainly an excellent instrument, to fix a man's attention and to inflame his ambition."* — **Steve Windsor** on John Adams.

Sorry, I had to. Let's move on. . .

I guess my point is, don't take this author stuff too seriously. Books have only made people fall in love, commit suicide, start wars, build bridges, save humanity . . . so, ya know, they aren't *that* important.

Because there's this. . .

> *"Writing is the most fun you can have by yourself."*
> — **Terry Pratchett**

Obviously this guy wasn't very creative, because there are so many things I could think of to. . . You know, I'm sensing I'm in enough trouble in this book, so I'm just not going there.

Anyway, did you feel that? I can tell you're starting to suck just a tiny bit less.

SUCK BUSTER:

Writing should be fun.

Take a step back and realize that writing can and is supposed to be . . . fun. **You get to be creative, write about topics you like and in general let your mind meander.** It's a stark contrast to the structured and rigid rules of most workplaces.

Sit down with your laptop or pen and paper and just let your mind wander a bit. **Write down whatever you want**. It doesn't have to make sense, it doesn't have to sell. . . I'm gonna go ahead and tell you that it doesn't even have to suck, because there is no suck, really. Just your words your way.

Go ahead, write yourself a note: "If I could write anything, any way I wanted, I would write about. . ."

It'll be fun.

ON A SIDE SUCK. . .

A couple quotes that just made me laugh out loud:

> *"English? Who needs that? I'm never going to England. Let's go get a smoke."* — **Homer Simpson**

> *"O God, O Venus, O Mercury, patron of thieves, lend me a little tobacco shop or install me in any profession, save this damn'd profession of writing, where one needs one's brains all the time."* — **Ezra Pound**

And these. . .

> *"My most important piece of advice to all you would-be writers: when you write, try to leave out all the parts readers skip."* — **Elmore Leonard**

> *"The dubious privilege of a freelance writer is he's given the freedom to starve anywhere."* — **S. J. Perelman**

Wait, that last one wasn't funny. . .

STEVE, YOU ARROGANT SUCK

ARROGANCE DOESN'T NECESSARILY SUCK

Honestly, I think this job takes at least a little bit of arrogance.

Think about it: You sit down with the intention of entertaining or informing another person with only your own perceived wisdom and/or wit? That takes a little brash and bold belief, don't you think?

These authors did. . .

> *"O you who in your wish to hear these things have followed thus far in your little skiffs the wake of my great ship that sails and sings, turn back and make your way to your own coast. Do not commit yourself to the main deep, for, losing me, all may perhaps be lost."* — **Dante Alighieri**

Um, I think he just said that everyone else sucked. Alluding to it is one thing, but this next guy doesn't mince words at all:

> *"Writing requires devotion and a bit of arrogance."*

— Buchi Emecheta

I'm not sure, but something in me really likes this next author a lot:

> *"I can write better than anybody who can write faster, and I can write faster than anybody who can write better."* — **A. J. Liebling**

The cockiness not doing it for ya? Okay, back to fear mongering, I guess.

FOCUSING YOUR SUCKING FEAR

A FEW MORE SUCK BUSTERS

Let's get a little deeper into what's behind your fear.

> *"I get a lot of letters from people. They say: 'I want to be a writer. What should I do?' I tell them to stop writing to me and get on with it."* — **Ruth Rendell**

Let go of perfectionism.

Fear doesn't end after you persuade yourself to become an author. Some of us edit and edit and edit, trying to get something perfect. That's most likely resistance to actually publishing in the form of fear. And what is publishing but giving the public the opportunity to determine if you suck or not?

Publish quickly and then revise and re-release. Don't let yourself get bogged down in endless editing.

Acknowledge your fears.

Fear's historical job was to keep you safe from physical harm. Understanding that can help you overcome it.

Realize that there's no injury that will come to you from writing. Carpal tunnel syndrome, maybe, but that just means you're writing a lot, getting better, sucking less.

Break your writing into its parts.

Focusing on the individual pieces—the steps in writing —can help you crowd out fear. Concentrating on and writing the next word, the next sentence, will stop you from viewing the entire process as a monumental and impossible task. **Complete each individual piece . . . and then move to the next.**

Lean into your fear.

I love a challenge and I love learning new skills. That has helped me overcome the fear to write. Because **fear is the flip side of the coin of exploration and adventure**. The quicker you learn that, the more fun you'll have writing.

Not enough depth?

Don't overcomplicate it.

Write, publish, rinse and repeat. Writing is as simple as that. Too often—I'm guilty of it in this book as well—we think of writing as too much hard work. And though it's difficult, I'm merely pointing out that winning takes work.

Is it impossible? Few things are. **Will it require effort? Yes.** Can you put forth the effort? That's not the question —anyone can. The question is, *will* you?

Okay, now let's take a look at all that hard work.

DARTH, HARD WORK SUCKS

MORE SUCKING QUOTES?

I'm gonna go all hypocritical-lazy right now. So, just quotes in this chapter. Okay, I just can't bring myself to be *that* lazy, so I'll add my two cents, of course.

Writing's hard work.

> "*The reward for hard work is the opportunity to do more.*" — **Darth Vader** hijacking **Jonas Salk**

Sometimes it sucks.

> "*I hate writing, I love having written.*" — **Dorothy Parker**

Suck it up and write!

> "*Beginning writers must appreciate the prerequisites if they hope to become writers. You pay your dues—which takes years.*" — **Alex Haley**

Embrace the pain.

"It is the purpose of literature to turn blood into ink." — **T. S. Eliot**

Be a professional.

"Only amateurs say that they write for their own amusement. Writing is not an amusing occupation. It is a combination of ditch-digging, mountain-climbing, treadmill and childbirth. Writing may be interesting, absorbing, exhilarating, racking, re-lieving. But amusing? Never!" — **Edna Ferber**

Pay your dues.

"Most people won't realize that writing is a craft. You have to take your apprenticeship in it like any-thing else." — **Katherine Ann Porter**

Surprise! More hard work.

"Being a writer is like having homework every night for the rest of your life." — **Lawrence Kas-dan**

Make writing part of your life.

"What I adore is supreme professionalism. I'm bored by writers who can write only when it's rain-ing." — **Noel Coward**

Get mean and get it done.

> *"Gimme a pickaxe, a shovel and a hard-top clay field . . . and I'll show you a ditch."* — **Steve Windsor** (Tweet this!)

The good news? There'll be no surprises in the afterlife.

> *"Writing is so difficult that I often feel that writers, having had their hell on earth, will escape all punishment thereafter."* — **Jessamyn West**

Writers . . . write.

> *"Writers don't have lifestyles. They sit in little rooms and write."* — **Norman Mailer**

Don't wait for inspiration.

> *"You can't wait for inspiration. You have to go after it with a club."* — **Jack London**

Never . . . ever . . . give up.

> *"A professional writer is an amateur who didn't quit."* — **Richard Bach**

Tired of worrying about sucking yet? Because I can do this all day. I will wear you down if I have to—if that's what it takes.

INSPIRATIONAL SUCK BUSTER:

This is an inspirational story about an unknown guy . . . and hard work.

I came across this story while researching this book and it struck me as having just about every element you need to believe, and then persevere in order to succeed. No superhumans that you can't relate to, no demigods of literature, but just a normal person . . . with a mission.

At 5'5", Brandon Todd took on an "impossible" mission: to be able to dunk a basketball. And do you want to know what he said about it? Why he did it? He wanted other kids who were short to believe it was possible. That's it.

> *"So much ridiculous training and hours and hours of running and jumping and throwing and stuff just to put a little basketball inside a cylinder that's ten feet off the ground. And it's still only worth two points."* — **Brandon Todd**

This is a fun one, because you get to watch a short indie flick. *FIVE/FIVE* is a film by Chris Jurchak and 522 Productions. The filmmakers were so inspired by Brandon that they decided to make the project with their own money.

"I'm willing to put myself through all this pain and anguish for that one moment to say, 'I can do it.'"
— **Brandon Todd**

It took him three years of failure . . . to train to dunk a basketball!

"Everybody fails. The only way to get to succeeding is to fail. It's just that simple." — **Brandon Todd**

Inspired by Russian powerlifters, Todd trained himself to dunk the ball through strength training, running and jumping exercises. He gained 85 pounds of muscle before he was finally able to dunk the ball.

"Anything's possible. Like anything. . . My grandfather and my mother used to tell me, 'Work hard, work hard, work hard.' And you're like, 'yeah, okay . . . nothing's happening.' And then boom!" — **Brandon Todd**

There'll always be enough people to tell you why something can't be done. Be the one who does it.

FIND YOUR OWN SUCKING PATH

THERE'S NO SUCKING "RIGHT" WAY

> *"A small daily task, if it be really daily, will beat the labors of a spasmodic Hercules."* — **Anthony Trollope**

There *is* no "right" way.

Ninety-day Novel, 1,000-2,000 words a day, *Novel in 30 Days*, the NaNoWriMo contest—30 days to 50k, *Write a Bestseller in Eight Hours* and my *Nine Day Novel* series. What do all of these "methods" have in common?

That's right—they're different. And that's the point—so are you.

The way you write will be the way that best fits you— your lifestyle, your physical location, your obligations, your marital status, your parental status, your habits, your motivation, your purpose in writing in the first place, and any other factor that's unique to you.

You shouldn't try to write the exact same way as another author any more than you should try to write in their voice, or wear someone else's underwear.

Writing is such a personal and solitary endeavor that only you can decide how best to do it. Everyone, and I mean *everyone*, offering you advice, including me, is doing exactly that—offering you their opinion on the matter. They—we—look at it from what works best for us, and then we try to help you figure out what will work best for you.

Make no mistake—it's opinion, not fact.

The reason I wrote the *Nine Day Novel* series in the first place was that the ever-present advice of "just write a little bit a day and in a couple years you'll have a novel" seemed like slow, waterboarding torture to me.

I believed that there was a section of the writing populace that was as sick and tired of getting no results—a physical first draft finished—as I was. Since I'd figured out a hardcore "method" to do just that, I wanted to share it with those people.

SUCK BUSTER:

By now, I'm hoping you realize that fear you're feeling has only ever been in your head. **To get rid of it, you need to simply decide that writing is much more important than not writing.** Once you finally make that switch, one of the first things you get to do is find a favorite place to write.

Your sacred space.

> *"I need solitude for my writing; not 'like a hermit'—that wouldn't be enough—but like a dead man."* — **Franz Kafka**

A coffeehouse, an office, a basement, on top of a mountain, a cabin. . . I've written in my car and finished a paragraph on the toilet.

I'm not saying that you should only write in your favorite spot, but you'll find that at times you need to escape to your sanctuary.

> *"Close the door. Write with no one looking over your shoulder."* — **Barbara Kingsolver**

Take a little time and explore a coffeehouse or library, or park bench. Or maybe you can find a room with a view. Writing is about connecting with the universe and your soul. Look around and notice places that appeal to you. Then open up your laptop or pad of paper and try a few spots out.

That place may just be the sacred space for your soul to let go and write.

SAYING ANYTHING . . . DOES NOT SUCK

John Cusack, arguably one of the most underrated Hollywood stars of the 80s, 90s, and 2000s, made a string of quirky, fun, and ultimately iconic films in the 1980s. Among them, one of my favorites—*Say Anything*.

In that movie, Cusack plays a meandering high school kid with a crush on a popular girl who seems to have everything going for her that he doesn't. Ultimately, the audience finds out that what's on the surface isn't necessarily the entire story. A great "novelic" lesson in and of itself, but not the point.

The thing that made the movie so awesome was Cusack's character and his charming ability to simply verbally vomit the thoughts from his mind.

No matter the time, no matter the place, no matter the social situation, he simply said the truth as it occurred to him. Some of it was nonsense, some was insane hilarity and some of it was simply pure, highly intuitive, devilishly daring, unfiltered, unabashed . . . genius truth . . . as he saw it.

I spent most of the first time I watched that movie riveted at what he might say next. What truth would he tell a girl's father who despised him? What truths would he tell the girl who knew only what the script of her life had in store for her? What truths would he tell someone who loved him but he didn't love back? Truths that mere mortals could not say—would not allow themselves to say—for fear of the consequences.

> *"The role of a writer is not to say what we can all say, but what we are unable to say."* — **Anaïs Nin**

Even just looking back on that film, I am reminded of what the essence of wanting to write and finding the courage to do it is all about. Anyone can follow the crowd by doing nothing, saying nothing, and being nothing that draws unwanted attention or criticism to themselves.

It takes raw courage and determination to continue in the face of machine-gun criticism, whose only goal is to make you shut your filthy, fornicating, fiction-flailing mouth!

And all of that . . . leads us to the critics.

CRITICISM . . . SUCKS

THE SUCKING HATERS. . .

> *"Asking a working writer what he thinks about critics is like asking a lamp post what it feels about dogs."* — **Christopher Hampton**

But the haters will show up.

Keep in mind that there will always be those who disagree and seek to make certain that you're aware of their disagreement. In short, they want to tell you how badly you suck . . . publicly.

I've found that writing criticism approaches religion in that regard. "If you don't believe as I do, I'll nail you to a cross or cut off your head. There, now do you believe me, infidel?" Uh, now I can't believe anything, because I'm dead.

> *"Literature is strewn with the wreckage of those who have minded beyond reason the opinion of others."* — **Virginia Woolf**

I have a love-hate-hate relationship with reviewers who

like to leave personal critiques instead of constructive book reviews. They love to hate me and I just hate them.

> *"God hates me."* — **Danny Glover** in *Lethal Weapon*
> *"Hate him back."* — **Mel Gibson** in *Lethal Weapon*

Uh-oh. . . I thought I was gonna make it through this book without any more rants. Dammit. . .

> *"Everybody does have a book in them, but in most cases that's where it should stay."* — **Christopher Hitchens**

I do *not* . . . like that guy. He's the kind of person that makes us all cringe before we even touch a finger to a keyboard. I picture him with a highball of straight scotch in his hand and a big smoldering cigar between the two fingers holding it, pretending that he likes the taste of them both.

Let me warn you: There are hundreds of MFA students graduating this year whose first work of creative literary "genius" will be a one-page, ego-slashing critique of the 400-page novel that you just wrote and self-published.

MARK TWAIN SUCKS?

> *"I haven't any right to criticize books, and I don't*

do it . . . except when I hate them. I often want to criticize Jane Austen, but her books madden me so that I can't conceal my frenzy from the reader; and therefore I have to stop every time I begin. Every time I read Pride and Prejudice I want to dig her up and beat her over the skull with her own shinbone." — **Mark Twain**

Even Mark Twain? Damn. . .

I think he's been using a pen name to review some of my books.

"I write to teach myself to endure criticism. It's a work in progress." — **Steve Windsor** (Tweet this!)

CAVEMEN KNEW HOW TO HANDLE SUCKING CRITICS

Back in the days of the caveman, if you complained about someone too loudly, an animal would hear the commotion and come along and eat you. Sadly, this is no longer the case.

All that conventional wisdom—motivational mushery to simply shrug off criticism—aside, here's the reality:

"From my close observation of writers ... they fall

into two groups: 1) those who bleed copiously and visibly at any bad review, and 2) those who bleed copiously and secretly at any bad review." — **Isaac Asimov**

Think about it: You bleed words for weeks, months, even years maybe. You finally get past the fear that you might suck and conjure the courage to press "publish." And then someone you don't know and will probably never meet, while you're sleeping soundly in the room down the hall, sneaks into your baby's nursery and sticks a knife in it.

Then they escape into the obscurity and anonymity of the Internet, hiding and hovering, looking for another baby to stab, going about their day as if they're reading the morning paper over coffee.

Sure, there are reviews that are helpful to you and readers, but I've found that the person giving constructive advice rarely gives it in the form of a one- or two-star review.

Three-star reviews are actually the working actors of reviews. There are critics who write helpful advice. And you can spot them because they usually find at least something constructive to say. **Don't discount a three-star review. Read it and fix what you can.**

You can usually find something to like about any book.

And yes, if you truly suck that badly, someone would've taken the time to inform you of it earlier. So let's just assume that you're doing the hard work that it takes to get better—suck less.

Telling someone else that they suck? Publicly? I have no idea how anyone does that. After putting my heart and soul into writing, I now understand my mother's advice that if you don't have anything nice to say, keep your filthy mouth shut!

Some say that the best you can do is to try to ignore bad reviews because the reaction is what a reviewer wants.

Those one-page critiques in review forums aren't to educate or assist anyone who might potentially read your book. They're written by a drunk who wants to stand up on a bar naked and say, "Hey, look at me! Aren't I clever and educated and stuff?" And afterward, they'll proceed to vomit all over some poor bystander's evening gown and laugh as if it were cute.

As an alternative perspective, you could adopt a . . . differing viewpoint. Possibly my entire motivation for writing this book:

> *"If you can't annoy somebody, there's little point in writing."* — **Kingsley Amis**

There's no sense in writing to please everyone. It simply can't be done.** It shouldn't be done. Go out to the bleeding edge, write the story you want to tell the best that you can, press publish, and then go write a better book.

Repeat those steps enough and eventually you'll learn to endure the people who simply can't stand you for getting out of bed in the morning, facing life head-on, refusing to put the barrel of a gun in your mouth, and having the absolute unabashed audacity to dare write a novel.

GET A SUCKING VOODOO DOLL

One- and two-star reviews are brutal. They can ruin your motivation if you don't handle them correctly.

Most other authors will give you "helpful" advice like "just ignore them," but I like to take a more . . . "active" approach.

SUCK BUSTER:

I keep a little **reviewer voodoo doll** on my computer desk (It's a Personalized Revenge Voodoo Doll) and a copious supply of needles in a little red pincushion that looks like an apple. There's a small container of chicken blood next to it. (I can't provide a link to the chicken blood.)

Each time I read a bad review—trivial tidbit, no author can resist reading them—I pick up my little voodoo doll, slowly stick a needle in the ear or the eye or, depending on my perceived nonsensical severity of the offense, the . . . uh, genitals of my little doll. Then I drip a little chicken blood on the wound to seal my unspoken deal with Kalfu. (Sorry, there's no "Devil" in Voodoo. Part of that "research" I was telling you about.)

Afterwards I say, "There there, Mrs. 'LoveCats' (because they always have some anonymous, ironic little Amazon handle like that), I'm sure that will heal up just fine. Juuuu-uust fine. . ." And then I go back to typing.

It works for me. Your mileage may vary with the technique.

I like to smile as I imagine that there's a certain person out there in anonymity-land who doubles over in pain, rushes to the doctor and neither of them can figure out why that person is bleeding profusely from their—whoa! I got a little carried away there.

But that's just me—I'm kind and forgiving like that.

You're gonna torture yourself over your bad reviews. But here's some more conventional advice:

Don't torture yourself. Call your therapist or author buddy, brew a fresh pot of coffee, poke your voodoo doll with a couple of pins, drip a little chicken blood and get back to writing.

> *"Unless a reviewer has the courage to give you unqualified praise, I say ignore the bastard."* — **John Steinbeck**

Don't, I repeat, do not respond to a bad review. That *is* some conventional wisdom I can open the car door, escort gently into the restaurant and slide out the chair at dinner for, because there's only one thing that pouring gasoline on a smoldering fire will do, and that is touch off an inferno!

SUCK BUSTER:

If it's impossible for you to ignore a review—you simply can't get past it—go read some of Chuck Wendig's one-star reviews. **Chuck's haters make yours look like kindergarteners at a drunken bar brawl.**

Go get a margarita, settle in at your computer, and go read Chuck's one- and two-star reviews on Amazon. They're guaranteed to desensitize you and put into perspective your fear of bad reviews.

And remember, there's always someone getting worse reviews than you are.

> *"The only time I'll get good reviews is if I kill myself."* — **Edward Albee**

And that's all I have to say about that.

Let's "immerse" ourselves in something a little more enjoyable, shall we?

SUCKING IS LIKE SEX

LADY GAGA SUCKING KNOWS. . .

> *"When you make music or write or create, it's really your job to have mind-blowing, irresponsible, condomless sex with whatever idea it is you're writing about at the time."* — **Lady Gaga**

Say what you will about her, she's right. **Rip off your filter like you tear off your lover's clothes at a hotel, and then write like you've never written before!**

Don't think Gaga's the only one:

> *"Writing is like sex. First you do it for love, then you do it for your friends, and then you do it for money."* — **Virginia Woolf**

And from the creator of *Firefly:*

> *"People love a happy ending. So every episode, I will explain once again that I don't like people. And then Mal will shoot someone. Someone we like. And their puppy."* — **Joss Whedon**

Not the kind of "happy ending" we were going for in this chapter, Joss, but I love *Firefly*, so you get to be in here anyway.

> *"Writing is a bit like sex—go a few days without it, and something just feels . . . off."* — **Steve Windsor** (Tweet this!)

Or something more pithy. . .

> *"Writing your first novel is like the first time you have sex. You have no idea what you're doing . . . but it feels incredible."* — **Anonym**—okay, that one was me again.

Enough fun. Back to serious.

AHHH, THE SUCKING MONEY

MONEY . . . DOES NOT SUCK

"If writers were good businessmen, they'd have too much sense to be writers." — **Irvin S. Cobb**

You don't have to live and die in obscurity before you start making some money. In fact, I've found that passive income from writing is some of the sweetest "coffee money" I've ever earned. So, if you're planning on writing for money, you're not alone. Bully for you!

It's time we stop telling people not to write for money. The advice-o-sphere is jam-packed with get-rich-quick books about how to write for money. There are two truths in that phenomenon:

One, **the blizzard of books on how to make money writing books makes finding a useful one difficult** at best. Two, those books wouldn't exist and sell so damn well if everyone and their brother and sister weren't gobbling them up like cupcakes in kindergarten.

So we can only assume that there are more than a few of us who are taking up writing with the goal of making a little money.

> *"I'd like to have money. And I'd like to be a good writer. These two can come together, and I hope they will, but if that's too adorable, I'd rather have money."* — **Dorothy Parker**

Sure, most of us know that people exchange money for value and our books will have to provide that—solve a problem or entertain a reader, which itself is just solving the problem of boredom. But let's stop glazing over the fact that that exchange happens in a free market society with the expectation that money will change hands.

> *"The exchange of money for value isn't evil. It's the delivery of less than perceived value that's the problem."* — **Steve Windsor** (Tweet this!)

Our solution to that is simple—write better books. So, in closing, we're back to sucking less for success.

The money will come. Concentrate on improving your writing. Because. . .

- Writers write.
- Authors get paid to write better.
- Rich authors get paid to write better than that.

- Wealthy authors got that way by marketing.

We'll talk about marketing in another book. Right now, all this talk about sucking has got me worn out. So I'm going to close with a few more quotes and put this sucking subject to bed.

I'M PLUMB OUT OF SUCK

JUST DO IT FOR SUCK'S SAKE

"You asked me about writing—how I did it. There is no trick to it. If you like to write and want to write, you write, no matter where you are or what else you are doing or whether anyone pays any heed. If you want to write about feelings, about the end of summer, about growing, write about it. A great deal of writing is not "plotted"—most of my essays have no plot structure, they are a ramble in the woods, or a ramble in the basement of my mind."
— **E. B. White**

"We are all apprentices in a craft where no one ever becomes a master." — **Ernest Hemingway**

And one final sucking sarcastic note:

"Writing is a sacred calling, but so are gardening, dentistry and plumbing, so don't put on airs. Writers are journalists before they're anything else. You keep coming back to journalism, which is continually hard work, to describe action, to narrate a sequence of events and somehow keep your own

fine sensibility out of it, to simply say how the game progressed.

"In all the best poems you find precise reporting, and this has very little to do with the mood of the writer. You can write comedy when you're sick, when you're lonely as a barn owl and your head hurts and your friends are mad at you. It's just work, that's all, and you go do it if you need to.

"It's a good life being a writer. Be grateful for it. And don't give advice to writers, no matter who asks you to." — **Garrison Keillor**

I lied, because in an oligarchy the "King" always gets the final word. (I'm not talking about Elvis.) I promised myself I wouldn't do it, but at the beginning of all this, I also said I was a hypocrite, so . . . here's the moment you've all been waiting for. **The almighty—*Stephen King!***

"The most important things are the hardest to say. They are the things you get ashamed of, because words diminish them—words shrink things that seemed limitless when they were in your head to no more than living size when they're brought out. But it's more than that, isn't it? The most important things lie too close to wherever your secret heart is buried, like landmarks to a treasure your enemies would love to steal away. And you may make reve-

lations that cost you dearly only to have people look at you in a funny way, not understanding what you've said at all, or why you thought it was so important that you almost cried while you were saying it. That's the worst, I think. When the secret stays locked within not for want of a teller but for want of an understanding ear." — **Stephen King**

And with that, I'm hoping that just a little bit of that sucking fear has "left the building."

NEXT SUCKING STEPS

SUCKING CONGRATULATIONS!

You've just survived this book on sucking. **By now you should realize three things: Your fear is real, we all have it, and the best way to get over it is to start writing.**

But don't get too serious about it, because some good-natured humor can cure a lot of that fear.

I had one goal with this book—show you that you're not alone in your fears about beginning a writing career. I wrote this book because I wanted to share a little bit of my personal journey and then show you how every author, at one time or another, has experienced your same fears. The only thing that separates you from them is that they decided to plow through their fear and write. It's really the only way.

By learning that self-doubt succumbs to action, you can overcome your fear and start writing.

The key is to take action. Commit to your goal of becoming an author. Decide today that you'll write your way through the fear.

Did this book do its job? If you're this far in, I'm betting it did.

When I started, I really didn't have high hopes for this book—I wrote it for fun. I know my style and voice grinds on some people. That's part of my own fear. But I also know that there are those budding authors out there who aren't motivated by reading the same advice, delivered the same way, over and over again, as a million variants on the same theme of nice-nice, happy-happy, joy-joy.

I like hard work.

There's a lot of hard work to becoming an author. Most people (marketers) know that you buy more stuff if they deliver that message in a cryptic little package labeled "working smarter not harder." Well, sometimes, there *is* no smarter, there's just harder.

That's my writer power—my "gift" if you will. I get down and dirty with the suck—banging out the word count—and I kick it's sucking ass. If I can prepare you to do that, I'm good with that. I'm all good. . .

There's a little gem in everything.

Everything we read as writers helps us learn and grow

and improve our writing—suck less. I truly believe that every book has at least one word of wisdom in it that helps us. I know I've tried to pour as many of those nuggets of hard-won wisdom into this book as I possibly could—my own and those of authors before me.

I bet you found at least one tidbit that made you smile, maybe even laugh. And that, coincidentally, is the key to overcoming fear.

So take the pieces of this book that you liked and use them to motivate you to tell your stories!

But, more importantly, learn all you can—learn what works for you. Then. . .

Do What Works!

Okay, just one more quote. I couldn't resist:

> *"Books and all forms of writing are terror to those who wish to suppress the truth."* — **Wole Soyinka**

What better reason to start writing than that!

JOIN THE SUCKFEST

I encourage you to **follow my progress as an author and get access to awesome tools** and how-to guides to use on your own author journey.

To entice you, Lise Cartwright and I wrote a free book for you, *29 Truths From the Trenches of Self-Publishing*.

You can get that book and get notified when our new authorship books come out, by clicking HERE. You can also visit http://authorbasics.com/lp1 and subscribe.

You can reach me here:
Email: steve@authorbasics.com

Other author how-to books in the *Nine Day Novel* series:

9 Day Novel: Authorphobia
9 Day Novel: Outlining
9 Day Novel: Writing
9 Day Novel: Self-Editing
9 Day Novel: Self-Publishing - coming in 2015
9 Day Novel: Book Marketing - coming in 2015
9 Day Novel: Writing a Series - coming in 2015

TEACHING YOU TO SUCK LESS

I realize that's not the best marketing tagline, but I vowed to follow the theme of this book to the bitter sucking end!

Author Coaching

Does it seem like it's taken your entire life to get your first novel out of your dreams and onto the page?

If you're like me, it took you forever to get up the courage to start writing. My first novel took me 27 years to write. I made every mistake a first-time author can make—but you don't have to.

After writing seven novels and publishing four of them, now I write faster, with more confidence and greater purpose than I ever have. They laughed at me when I said I would do it, but the draft of my fourth novel took me literally nine days.

I believe in the power of writing. That's why I'm committed to helping first-time authors get their drafts out of their heads and into readers' hands with as little time and struggle as possible.

I'll help you master the three things you have to as an author:

1. Overcoming the belief that you're not "allowed" or "good enough" to write.

2. Learning the mechanics and structure of storytelling.

3. Navigating the technological environment of writing, editing, packaging and physically publishing your first novel.

If you're tired of "aspiring" to become an author and are ready to finally publish your first book, contact me and let's get started!

Email: steve@authorbasics.com

ABOUT THE SUCKING AUTHOR

HOW DOTH I SUCK?

Steve Windsor was born in Augsburg, Germany to U.S. military parents. So he doesn't know a bit of German.

I'm just a guy who decided to write one day. And roughly two years and two million words into it, I've learned so much and my writing has improved so much. . . But it all came at a cost in time and frustration. I've bled words.

One of the things I related to a recent interviewer was that if you find the thing that will make you deny sleep, food, bathroom breaks, even sex . . . then that is your true calling. Mine is to write and help other authors overcome their fears and grow their writing "muscle."

My belief is that I have information you need to avoid some of the frustration and pain that I suffered in starting up my dream. And simply put, I want to write books for you because of it.

The fiction I write is hard and raw and my non-fiction is even harder. I don't like to mince words.

I like heroes and villains just about the same, because a good villain usually has a bad backstory that isn't really his or her fault. Sure you gotta kill them, but realize you're going to be a little sad about it, too.

Andrew Vachss is my hero. You should definitely read his novels. And I love George R.R. Martin because he's not afraid to kill a hero.

I'm here to help you grow as an author. The best way you can do that—go write something!

— Steve Windsor
Best-Selling Author & Writing Coach

TEDDY NEEDS YOUR HELP!

Thank you for reading this book!

I've done everything I can to jerk you out of your fear of writing. By now, you realize that I believe in order to succeed at writing—suck less—you have to have no fear. No filter. No limits.

To further prove that, let me introduce you to Teddy. He is one of 27 "reviewers" that I keep in my own personal reviewer sweatshop. Isn't he cute?

Anyway, "Teddy" gets a little jar of liquified peaches on his breaks. He only *gets* those breaks when someone *else* leaves a review.

Won't you give Teddy a break? Click HERE to leave a review—give Teddy a break. He needs it. Thanks so much! Steve - Teddy's sucking boss

www.ingramcontent.com/pod-product-compliance
Lightning Source LLC
Chambersburg PA
CBHW070906290526
45795CB00001B/228